"Master the lessons in this book, and all your partnerships will improve...."

—James A. Autry, author of *Love and Profit* and *Life and Work*

"It's invigorating to read about real-life customer partnerships. Chip Bell makes them practically rhapsodic."

—Michael Pellecchia, Syndicated Book Reviewer

"Five stars and a thumbs up for *Customers As Partners!* If you want customers for life, this book has the secrets."

—George Dean Johnson, Jr., President, Blockbuster Entertainment

---

"Chip rings the bell with *Customers As Partners.* I find myself re-reading sections and quoting from it frequently."

—Van Skilling, Executive Vice President, TRW Information Systems

---

"I've made *Customers As Partners* required reading for every member of our staff. It's a beautifully written book that shows what it takes to develop lasting partnerships with your customers. "

—Mike Kutka, Editor, *Temp Digest*

"*Customers As Partners* is full of wisdom, inspiration, and joy... a valuable gift to the corporate world."

"Chip Bell has captured the essence of what good solid business is all about, partnering with customers... and he has done so in a book that reads like a well-written, light-hearted novel."

"If your company wants to take a giant step, from being a superior service provider to establishing lifelong partnerships with your customers, this book is a must. We have made it required reading (and practice) for all employees."

"*Customers As Partners* is a practical, inspiring guide.... Bell provides step-by-step guidelines in a down-home manner that keeps the reader realistically motivated."

"It is easy to recommend *Customers As Partners* to anyone interested in creating meaningful, long-term customer connections. It serves as a fine primer for neophytes, as well as a rich source of food for thought for more advanced partnership architects."

—Theodore B. Kinni, President, The Business Reader

"Partnerships are what great customer service is all about. In *Customers As Partners,* Chip Bell explains how to achieve success by creating partnerships, caring for them, and helping them grow."

—Dave Thomas, founder of Wendy's, and author of *Dave's Way*

"*Not* building relationships based on customer needs, rapport, and trust has sounded the death knell for many a company. Chip Bell's book will help your customers become delighted, long-term fans."

—Richard C. Bartlett, Vice Chairman, Mary Kay Corporation and author of *The Direct Option*

"*Customers As Partners* offers an in-depth and intimate look at what genuine customer service is about."

—Peter Block, author of *Stewardship, The Empowered Manager,* and *Flawless Consulting*

CUSTOMERS ◆AS◆ PARTNERS

BUILDING RELATIONSHIPS THAT LAST

Chip R. Bell

Berrett-Koehler Publishers
San Francisco

Berrett-Koehler Publishers, Inc.
155 Montgomery Street
San Francisco, CA 94104-4109
Tel: (415) 288-0260 Fax: (415) 362-2512

ORDERING INFORMATION
Individual sales
Special discounts are available on quantity purchases by corporations, associations, and others. For details, contact the "Special Sales Department" at the Berrett-Koehler address above.

Orders for college textbook/course adoption use
Please contact Berrett-Koehler Publishers at the address above.

Orders by U.S. trade bookstores and wholesalers
Please contact: Publishers Group West
4065 Hollis Street, Box 8843, Emeryville, CA 94662
Tel: (510) 658-3453; 1-800-788-3123 Fax: (510) 658-1834

Printed in the United States of America
Printed on acid-free and recycled paper that is composed of 85% recovered fiber, including 15% post-consumer waste.

Library of Congress Cataloging-in-Publication Data
Bell, Chip R.
    Customers as partners: building relationships that last / Chip R. Bell
        p. cm.
    Includes bibliographical references and index.
    ISBN 1-881052-78-8 (alk. paper)
    1. Customer service. 2. Customer relations. I. Title
    HF5415.5.B434 1994
    658.8'12--dc20   94-16999
                                                                      CIP

First Hardcover Printing: July 1994
First Paperback Printing: January 1996
    99 98 97 96   10 9 8 7 6 5 4 3
This paperback edition contains the complete text of the original hardcover edition.

A BARD&STEPHEN BOOK
AUSTIN, TEXAS

Copyediting: **Jeff Morris**
Proofreading: **Jamie Fuller**
Text Design: **Suzanne Pustejovsky**
Composition/Production: **Jeff Morris**
Index: **Linda Webster**

To
the major Bells
in
my life —
Nancy,
Bilijack,
Ray,
and Avis

TABLE OF CONTENTS

Contents

Howdy, Partner

(Please don't skip this part!)

MY GRANDDADDY AND I WOULD occasionally go fishing in one of several ponds that peppered his Georgia farm. A pond in Georgia is any body of water bigger than a creek and smaller than a lake. Stocked with fish from the outset — in our case big-mouthed bass, trout, and bream — these dammed-up springs served as a major source of water for irrigation and for cattle during long seasons of drought.

We fished from a small wooden rowboat my cousin Roger had made in shop class at Patterson High School. We fished with cane poles, lead sinkers, small corks, and worm-laden hooks. Granddaddy would typically pull in five fish to my one. "How come I'm not gettin' any fish?" I would usually ask in frustration. Silence followed. Then, several minutes later, as if I had just asked the question, he'd turn one eye my way and drawl: "That's 'cause you aren't holdin' your mouth right!"

For a long time I took him literally. I'd contort my mouth into a variety of shapes in a valiant attempt to find the proper facial expression for maximum fish extraction.

One summer day I finally gave up and asked him what he meant, because I wasn't figuring it out on my own! It turned out to be a major boon to "bringing in a mess," as we called the act of catching a sufficient quantity of "keepers" for a family-sized fish fry. "Holding your mouth right" meant an array of things that included sitting still; not making noises; keeping a watchful eye on the cork; setting the hook when the fish, with a mouthful of worm, pulled the cork underwater; playing out enough line; and a hundred and one other fishing nuances.

What is this book like?

I want you to know early on how to "hold your mouth right" — to get the most from this book. That is the goal of this preface. The style of this book is anecdotal and emotional — just like partnerships. It also may be helpful for you to know a little about how I organized this book. That way you can more quickly enter into the pace without jolt or confusion. The messages and methods may otherwise appear oblique — and you'll feel something akin to the feeling I had as a youngster fishing with my granddaddy.

Chapters start either with a story followed by key principles and some discussion and "how to's," or with a few key principles followed by a story or stories for illustration and discussion. Highly logical, analytical readers: Beware! You will be tempted to hopscotch the stories to get right to the bare bones of the matter. I encourage you not to. You may save time — but bones without heart will fail to offer you the living learnings that are the essential truths of partnering.

What is this book about — and not about?

*T*his book is *not* about forming strategic alliances or crafting a partnership in a legal sense of the word. There are plenty of books on that subject. This book is also not about how to give customers good service. That subject has also been the focus of many books.

Customers as Partners is about taking "customerships" to a higher level of union than the traditional service-provider-to-consumer relationship. It is about developing a kinship that nurtures commitment and cultivates loyalty.

This book can *enrich* strategic alliances and all customer-service encounters. It is always helpful to remember that long before contracts, price negotiation, and the sound of a cash register, there were people seeking people to respond to a need. Too often, customer disdain or indifference is born not from the logical aspect of the association but from the psycho-logical (the logic of people) dimension of the relationship. The human side of service is the substance of this book.

Not all customer encounters need to be partnerships. I get great service at the local car wash. But for the attendant to be friendly, functional, and fast is enough for me. The same is true for excellent service from the Federal Express or UPS delivery person. I see these encounters as neither a relationship nor a partnership.

What are the payoffs for powerful partnerships?

*C*ustomer partnership is first an attitude! It is an orientation that starts with a deep and assertively demonstrated respect for the customer, moves with the spirit of contribution, and ends with the joy of knowing the best possible has been done to meet or exceed a need.

The emotional merits of customer partnerships are important. There are also economic rewards. Frederick Reichheld and W. Earl Sasser Jr., in the September–October 1990 issue of *Harvard Business Review,* reported that the longer a customer remains your fan, the more money she spends with you. The credit card customer worth $30 a year after one year is worth $55 in year five. The average industrial laundry customer jumps from an initial annual worth of $144 to $256 in his fifth year of loyal patronage. The auto-service customer who brings the company $25 annual profit will be generating $88 by the fifth year. Customer loyalty pays and pays and pays.

One way service providers foster customer loyalty is through the creation of a customer partnership. Customer partnership is a primary ingredient in the Nordstrom–Federal Express–Lexus formula for turning satisfied customers into converted champions who daily act as advocates. Partnership evidence is manifest in customer comments like "I've been going there for years" and "I wouldn't go anywhere else."

Who should read this book?

I wrote this book primarily for two groups: people who deal directly with customers and people who supervise, manage, or lead others in a service-sensitive work environment. I hope the book will also be useful to customers. After all, they form the other side of the partnership.

A few friends have suggested that anyone anywhere who has an interest in effective relationships (partnerships) would find this book useful. They also said I was handsome, smart, a great cook, and a fantastic host! Aren't friends wonderful? You be the judge. And if you like this book, recommend it to those you think would find it beneficial.

If you prefer customer encounters to remain perfunctory, superficial, or "at arm's length," put this book back on the shelf for someone else to buy. If you enjoy customer experiences that are memorable because of the way customers react when they get a committed connection along with a commodity or service — welcome! Or if you like cultivating a rapport with customers that causes them to feel like family or to promote your service to all who will listen, this book will give you a philosophy, several perspectives, and countless techniques.

How to get the most from this book

A couple of additional suggestions for getting the maximum benefit from this book: think about the key partnerships in your life. What makes them work or not work? I typically think about my wife, my son, and my business partners. How can your life-partnership successes and failures instruct you in partnerships with customers, suppliers, and colleagues? If your customer were your best friend, how would you serve that customer? What do you want from customer relationships? Do you want lifelong customers? Or are you more interested in short-term, largely pleasant, but mostly functional customer relationships? Do you want your customers to think of you with some level of admiration, devotion, or loyalty?

Another suggestion: when you finish a chapter, stop and think about it. I know — I don't either! We all wonder when life will reach a point where "slowing down" will be doable and lovable, and not guilt inducing! But try to pull off on a mental side track and reflect on how you might use the concepts from each chapter. I think you will gain a lot more by so doing.

The design of the book cover was a careful choice aimed at symbolically conveying the spirit of partnership. The "amber waves of grain" in the background are intended to communicate a feeling of abundance, harvest, and growth. The "spacious skies" (with a few clouds) signify the visionary, forward-thinking, yet realistic aspect of successful partnerships. The type style on the cover and throughout the book was selected for its boldness, clarity, and symmetry — all important dimensions of relationships at their best.

They say we find our life examples where we live. As a service-quality consultant, I find mine on the road. Consequently, I've drawn a lot of illustrations from hotels, airlines, taxicabs, and restaurants. I believe the issues are the same, so the lessons learned have broad relevance.

I hope you are already *experiencing* a sense of partnership from this book. I want to be a partner with you — author to reader. I promise not to come home with you, or ask you questions that are too personal or embarrassing. But I would ask a favor of you: when you finish this book, let me know what you think of it. My address is on the last page of the book.

This trip we will be taking together is one I hope you will find fun, useful, and spirit-full ("spirit-full" is a word I made up to mean "full of spirit and passion"; I'll be making up a lot of words between here and the last page). I wrote this book because I have too often experienced good customer service that lacked depth and soul. I have frequently thought, "If this service provider made a slight change in attitude, attention, or attribute, this good service could be awesome." I have too frequently witnessed customers for the moment who would enthusiastically become customers for life if given an opportunity.

If this book works as intended, you will experience a range of emotions. You may get a little misty-eyed from time to time. I hope you chuckle a lot! Mostly, I hope you stop periodically and reprogram what you have thought, believed, or felt about customer service and customer partnerships. My hope is that you will discover many insights and find opportunities for reflection.

After reading this book, don't be surprised if you become a customer with higher expectations. Customer partnerships can yield such a different quality of experience that we want more. Like freedom tasted for the first time by citizens of a formerly communist country, it may become difficult to get it back into the box! Service providers in your path may find you a more assertive consumer, intent on getting only the best.

So as you enter the doors of customer partnership, be clear about whom you want by your side. This book is dedicated to those you hope will join you.

xv

" *The sole meaning of life is to serve humanity.* "

— Leo Tolstoy

PARTNERSHIP IS...

*** The highest destiny of the individual is to serve rather than to rule. ***

— Albert Einstein

Partnership . . .

The word is spoken with such ease, and
  pictures parade before our mind's eye.
We scan this collage in search of meaning
  in this concept deserving of softer syllables.

We see a picture of colleagues,
  their letters speaking their story . . .
Inc., P.A., Ltd., and Associates.
We see a picture of couples,
  their rings telling their theme . . .
dearly beloved, oh promise me, I do.
We see a picture of alliances,
  their photos narrating their news . . .
CEO 1 shakes hands with CEO 2.

But what does partnership mean?

After the business cards are printed,
  and the wedding cake is cut,
  and the boardroom is silent . . . what's left?

Partnership is a bond of kindred spirits
  seeking
a setting for truth,
a context for trust, and
a crucible for generosity.

Partnership is a verb disguised as a noun.
It is a force released, "un-nouned,"
  when dreams connect
and service is gracefully given.

Chapter 1

THE ANATOMY OF CUSTOMER PARTNERSHIP

RICHARD MCCOY has done my taxes for fifteen years. Though we've never said the words, we are partners in the matter of making the Bell family financially whole and free from worry. Our partnership is one in which we each have a mutual interest in a successful relationship. Richard calls me his client and refers to his actions on my behalf as assisting, supporting, and advising. He reminds me quarterly to send in my estimated tax payment; I send him articles on how to manage a small business practice. Richard never acts deferential or arrogant; he is always respectful and smart.

The seventeen-year-old part-time employee at the supermarket I frequent (Himynameis Bill) treats me like a king! He rushes to bag my groceries, always puts the bread on top, and acts surprised — and very pleased — when I tip him every week. Bill calls me "sir" and graciously defers to my whims ("Could you put those four items in a separate bag?"). He never acts tired or bored, which I'm sure he must sometimes feel. Bill always acts eager to please and respond.

These are two examples of excellent customer service: the customer as partner and client, and the customer as king and consumer. Each is appropriate in its own context, and not likely interchangeable. I would want neither a CPA who acted like Bill nor a supermarket clerk who tried to treat me with the kind of professional equality I get from Richard. However, these two models cover only a few of the many possible service relationships.

4

What kind of customer relationship do you expect of your banker, the concierge at the hotel, your auto mechanic, your hairdresser? Do you expect these relationships to be the same intimate partnerships you have with your doctor, lawyer, and CPA? When do you seek the highly deferential actions you usually get from the grocery-store clerk, refrigerator-repair person, or the neighborhood kid who mows your lawn?

The path to customer loyalty

*C*ustomer satisfaction is no guarantee of customer retention. We can all remember times we switched vendors, merchants, or service providers with no dissonance, disdain, or disappointment, simply because we found someone else to provide that service who was a bit more convenient, more responsive, less expensive, or just different. We were not dissatisfied. We also were not particularly delighted. They were there, getting the job done, and then we switched.

What causes customers to demonstrate loyalty? Sometimes it can come from one extraordinary, dazzling experience. As a professional partner, Richard dazzles me; but then, so does Himynameis Bill. But with the Bill-type service, my allegiance is likely to remain as long as the dazzlement happens often enough. Yet dazzlement, while great, is not likely to be sustainable. If our marriages depended on turning in a premier performance on a perpetual basis, most of us would not make it beyond the glow of the honeymoon! The long-term quality is due mainly to a special bond or relationship — a partnership.

5

Demonstrating a partnership attitude

What is a customer partnership? If you strip out the contracts, covenants, and deals, what do you have left? A customer partnership is a living demonstration of an attitude or orientation.

◆ Powerful partnerships are anchored in an attitude of generosity, a "giver" perspective that finds pleasure in extending the relationship beyond just meeting a need or requirement.

◆ Powerful partnerships are grounded in trust. Partners don't spend energy looking over their shoulders, but instead take a leap of faith and rely on the relationship.

◆ Powerful partnerships are bolstered by a joint purpose. While this purpose is rarely "written down," each partner is enfolded in a vision or dream of what the association could be and a commitment to take the relationship to a higher plane.

◆ Powerful partnerships are coalitions laced with honesty. Truth and candor are seen as tools for growth rather than devices for disdain. Partners serve each other straight talk mixed with compassion and care.

◆ Powerful partnerships are based on balance. Their pursuit of equality, however, is one that seeks stability over time rather than absolute encounter-to-encounter equilibrium.

◆ Powerful partnerships are grounded in grace. The spirit of partnership has an artistic flow that gives participants a sense of familiarity and ease.

More customer relationships need to be managed toward the Richard end of the continuum. Effective customer partnerships can keep customers returning, through thick and thin, for better or worse, in good times and bad. Effective customer partnerships have qualities that can ensure their success. These are the qualities the service provider must initiate, demonstrate, or replicate.

While the concept of customer partnership generally implies a long-standing relationship, the *feeling* of partnership may be created in the short-term relationship. Arising in part from the service provider's focus on creating a high-value service experience, this quality of *service intimacy* requires a commitment to extraordinary giving based solely on the hope (but not the requirement) that it will be rewarded with reciprocal customer devotion to the service provider. Stated differently, it is a combination of "love at first sight" with service altruism in its highest form. It is an attitude of unconditional serving.

A few partnership warnings

A few caveats about partnerships. First, all partnerships, whether with colleague, customer, or spouse, require a more complete, deeper commitment, have more stringent requirements, and take more work than transient or temporary customer relationships.

Dr. Marcia Glass is my physician. After each "fix something" visit, she calls me to see how I'm doing. She always builds extra time into my office visits to sit and chat about my family and work, and about hers. Does she see fewer patients that way? I'm sure she does. But I can assure you I have never had a doctor I would more enthusiastically recommend than Dr. Glass. And I always follow her "take *all* the medicine" instructions, even after I think I'm well.

Second, not all customers want to participate in customer partnerships. Some customers enjoy a degree of mystery, privacy, and aloofness. As the service relationship becomes more intense and intimate, they flinch and move on to another service relationship with exit language that says, "They knew us too well. . . . We needed some breathing room." Other customers desire the "serve me" relationship. They enjoy the deference of the service provider but prefer not to reciprocate the effort. Hotel guests who came to be pampered might rave about the service, but would recoil in disdain if they were expected to demonstrate their loyalty by helping to create the extraordinary experience.

Given all that, are customer relationships that are more like partnerships worth the extra effort they require from you? You bet! Not only are customer partnerships more economically rewarding, they can endure more mistakes (be more forgiving) and produce greater intrinsic rewards than traditional service-provider-to-customer encounters.

What makes customer partnerships work?

An effective customer partnership can be dissected many ways, and the labels for their parts can be diverse. I have elected to include in this book's anatomy of customer partnerships six qualities or attributes essential to successful partnerships: abundance, trust, dreams, truth, balance, and grace. Each section of this book contains several chapters that examine these qualities or attributes in depth.

I have elected to phrase the six qualities in somewhat antique words. For instance, instead of describing "reliability" or "assurance," I chose "trust." "Truth" is a deeper word than "candor" or "honesty"; "dreams" has implications that words like "mission" or "purpose" do not. The goal is not to be semantically pure in the choice of labels, but to be instructive and insightful in the word pictures the labels evoke.

8

Abundance

Powerful partnerships start with an attitude of abundance or generosity. Partners don't keep score! The noncompetitive nature of an effective partnership means that each partner approaches the relationship believing *not* that there is a finite quantity of benefit to be derived, but that increased contribution to the relationship causes it to grow and prosper. As with love (the more you give, the more there is), service providers who harbor an abundance mentality, as Stephen Covey calls it, act as if there were always plenty for both themselves and the customer. Partners are not overly concerned with distribution: they trust that things will even out over the long haul. Partners know that the synergy of their combined efforts creates abundance; bounty is a product of working together. There is more, not less, to go around as a result of the partnered effort.

Trust

Great partnerships are based on a sense of trust that leaves partners feeling confident. Trust is a quality associated with reliability, assurance, and faith. Trust lends credence to a partner's word. To be trustworthy (that is, worthy of trust), one must have a track record of fidelity. Partners count on each other. My friend Larry Davis defines trust as "a state of readiness for unguarded interaction with someone or some thing." Partners waste no time or energy looking over a shoulder or worrying that a promise made or implied will become a promise broken or ignored. Such experience fosters confidence to reach further; tightropes and tight situations can be assertively traversed with the net of trust beneath them.

Dreams

Effective partnerships enjoy shared visions or aims. Their analogous hopes foster harmony and balance. Mutuality starts with distant views in unity rather than close-up requirements in common. The word "partner" implies individual parts that share for mutual gain. While gains need not be the same, there is an expectation that each "part" will make a contribution valued by the other "part." A collaborative vision is the crucible in which parts are mixed for results favored by the "owners" of each part.

Truth

The truth-seeking component of effective partnership is that which values candor and openness. It is the dimension that honors authenticity and realness. The path to truth in relationships is replete with interpersonal risk taking and mutual critique. It involves the courage to ask for feedback as well as the compassion to give feedback. Truth may sometimes leave relationships temporarily uncomfortable and bruised, but truth always leaves partnerships hearty and healthy. It is the quality that exterminates guilt and deceit. Truth nurtures cleanness in associations.

Balance

As kids sharing a candy bar, we had a back-seat rule: whoever divided the candy bar got second pick on which half he ate. The quest was for equity and fairness. When choosing sides for playground athletics, we used various rituals to ensure parity. The "play fair" side of effective partnerships includes a focus on equality — not the type that necessarily requires actual fifty-fifty, but rather one that causes each affected party to assess joint dealings as *10* balanced, the outcomes as fair.

Grace

Spend time with couples who have great marriages and you come away with a new appreciation for peace and tranquility. The same is true with parents who are fortunate enough to have solid relationships with their children. While there may be occasional uproars, infrequent pressured encounters, and intermittent conflicts, the norm is calm and composure. There is an ease and repose that I will label "grace."

Each of these six sections is introduced by a poem that I crafted to capture the essence of the partnership attribute. You already met the first poem a few pages back. I shifted from prose to poetry to communicate that partnership at its best is artistic — more heart than head, more romantic than rational.

Are there only six attributes to customer partnerships? Of course not. Partnerships are growing entities that perpetually change. However, if you assertively manage the truth, trust, grace, and balance dimensions in customer relationships with an attitude of abundance reaching toward the hope of your collective dreams, then the parts this book misses are likely to be unimportant.

Partnerships are the expectancy of the best in our abilities, attitudes, and aspirations. Partnerships are far more than good synergy. Synergy means that the whole is greater than the sum of the parts. All partnerships are synergistic, but great partnerships go beyond "greater than" to a realm of unforeseen worth.

There is an expression in golf: "playing over your head." It means that a player is playing at an unexplained level of excellence in which the serendipitous and the extraordinary seem the momentary norm. Great partnerships are relationships in which two or more people are "serving over their heads."

66 *No person was ever honored for what he received. Honor has been the reward for what he gave.* 99
— Calvin Coolidge

Chapter 2

THE SPIRIT OF CUSTOMER PARTNERSHIP

WHATEVER HAPPENED to Leroy Clark? Mr. Clark was the grocer in my South Georgia home town. He was my introduction to what it meant to be a "merchant" — courteous and eager to help all who came into his small, all-purpose store. His style bore no resemblance to the style of Shakespeare's Venice-based merchant, the one debated hotly in Mrs. Wilcox's sophomore English class — Mr. Clark would never *think* of demanding a "pound of flesh," even from the most ruthless customer!

Today the corporate world is rediscovering the sense of service that permeated Leroy Clark's bones. This rediscovery is made to sound like a major breakthrough — something absent from the past, newly found and terribly important. Every business journal seems to parade superior customer service almost the way *Life* covered the 1969 walk on the moon. The Leroy Clarks get no credit for using methods now attributed to Disney, Ritz Carlton Hotels, Federal Express, Nordstrom, and the like.

What happened between the early-1950s version of small-town service and the present-day renaissance of that same orientation? How did the business world move so far away from Leroy Clark, and why is his brand of customer service so sought? Can it be that Leroy could teach us lessons about '50s service relevant to the '90s?

Before you chide me about superior service being much more than neighborly manners, let me quickly add that Leroy Clark knew a lot about service vision, customer-friendly delivery systems, service recovery, and front-line empowerment. To be sure, Leroy was no scholar of service management nor a graduate of customer-relations training classes. He did what he did out of a solid grounding in the premise that serving implied a partnership with the customer. Service to Leroy was about reciprocal power — his power to provide goods and services coupled with the customer's power to keep him in business.

He was clear on his role — to provide groceries and a few small appliances to a small, rural community. He didn't get hung up on "being the best" or "improving the bottom line." He gave no thought to franchising, diversifying, merging, or acquiring. He simply provided groceries to his neighbors at a fair price. He did not have to remind himself to "stick to his knitting" or "stay close to his customers." He had few pretensions, aspired to no baronial or congressional status, and had few managerial tools to lead him astray. Leroy was a merchant, and that was that. He demonstrated a responsibility to those who crossed the threshold of his grocery store.

Leroy acted out of a simple belief: "My customers are my partners and neighbors." To cheat, disappoint, or

14

dissatisfy a customer would be as inappropriate as starting a heated argument at a family reunion. And he would no more question the honesty of a customer than he would accuse one of his two daughters of stealing. They were his partners in the world of enterprise. He believed that his customers were honest — and they always seemed to be. He also assumed that differences with customers would be resolved with a sense of fair play — and they always seemed to be.

Leroy knew what his customers needed and expected. One day my father, a full-time banker *and* full-time farmer, stopped in to buy a loaf of bread. "Mr. Bell," said Leroy in his always polite voice, "I ordered you some of those fly strips for your pig house. Last time you were in here, you mentioned that the flies were about to take away your new farrowing house." I wonder how many service organizations would stock an item based solely on data gathered through eavesdropping or "fair weather" conversation. Leroy cared a lot more about service than inventory. And when my father opted *not* to buy the sticky, yellow fly strips, Leroy acted neither hurt nor disappointed. He knew his role and responsibility — and he fulfilled both.

Leroy rearranged his grocery store every year or so. "Customers are forever telling me better ways to set up the store," he said one midsummer day when I was in town to buy a lawnmower blade at Hinson's Hardware and stopped by the New City Market to buy a Forever Yours candy bar and an RC cola. "I'm not always real crazy about their ideas," he admitted, "but if I didn't make a few changes, they'd think I didn't have any respect for 'em." And if there was a new fad, Leroy would have it in a hurry. He had hula hoops and fire balls before the big stores in Macon had them!

Today we marvel at the superstar companies that make a fetish of listening and responding to customers — 3M, USAA, GE Answering Center, Stew Leonard's. Leroy knew how to listen; he also knew how to convince his customers that their input was valued and respected. Oh, I realize it's much easier with one store and a stable customer base. But I'll bet Leroy would have figured out how to listen dramatically if he'd been the president of The Great Atlantic and Pacific Tea Company! It was in his nature to pay attention to those he served.

Though I dare say he'd never heard the word in his whole life, Leroy was a master at empowerment — especially at empowering his only stock boy. Working hard one day to open a case of butter beans, the young man was embarrassed by a cruel racial slur thrown at him by a couple of loud white teenagers. "You don't have the brains of a . . . ," they rudely jeered. Leroy calmly walked over to the rowdy boys and demanded they leave. Before they were out of earshot, he turned to the stock boy and said, "Adel, I'm going to the bank. You know what to do, so you're in charge of the store while I'm gone."

16

Now, that's small potatoes in today's high-rise corporate world. But in a very conservative, racially biased Georgia country town in the early 1950s, it was empowerment with a capital E. Adel went into the Navy after high school, then on to a small college. I think he's selling real estate somewhere in the Midwest and doing rather well.

I'm not saying Leroy was a saint without prejudice. But Leroy knew that the stock boy would probably get more "can-you-help-me-find" questions than he would. And he knew that if this young man were treated with respect and importance, he would more likely exhibit confidence and competence when serving a customer. What would Leroy think today if he knew his leadership practices were the goal of senior executives who are paid more in a year than Leroy earned in a lifetime?

Leroy was also effective at recovering from a customer service breakdown. There was no need for a written, published "service guarantee" — Leroy *was* the guarantee. He would not even consider a mere discount if something the customer purchased was not up to her expectations. "You don't owe me a thing" would always take precedence over "Three dollars off if it's late." We need more Leroys instead of merchants who too frequently argue over an eighty-nine-cent carton of milk with a customer who, if loyal to that same store, will spend forty thousand dollars over the average eight years she lives in a given location.

Leroy also knew that if any of his customers had a problem, his initial focus had to be on fixing first that customer — then the customer's problem. My grandmother once bought an ice-cream churn from Leroy — the kind grandsons endlessly hand crank to turn cold, thick cream into a summer eve's delight. It was a hot July day when she first unpacked it only to discover the crank was missing. "Leroy," she complained over the phone, "you sold me a bum steer!" Well, Leroy drove three miles into the country with another churn. With him he brought a fresh-baked apple pie and two gallons of "store-bought" ice cream. Now, here is the best part: he sat out in the shade for a half hour with my grandmother, quizzing her on her secrets for getting azaleas to grow big and healthy!

I suppose I'm on thin ice implying that it's possible to simplify a very challenging issue. A few of the many complex barriers to replicating Leroy's brand of customer partnerships include corporate bigness, bureaucracy, legal restrictions, diverse customer requirements, increased competition domestically and internationally, scarcity of committed and competent service employees, etc., etc., etc. And if it were as easy now as it was in South Georgia then, great service books would not become best sellers, nor would corporations hire service-quality consultants to help them figure out ways to enhance the customer's experience of service.

Yet sometimes I wonder if it really is simpler than we realize. Perhaps we just need to rekindle and nurture the passion that guided Leroy Clark to treat customers like partners. It's possible I am just a romantic opting for nostalgia instead of accepting the cold reality of the present.

But then again, maybe not.

"The roots of happiness grow deepest in the soil of service."

— John-Roger, coauthor of *Life 101*

ABUNDANCE

abundance *n*. 1. An
extremely plentiful or
oversufficient supply.
2. Overflowing fullness.

Gift vs. Greed

I surprise, I delight, their response I enjoy;
    You're a fool if you think life is fair.
I provide, I get high on the joy in my heart;
    You're naive if you think they will care.

But the greedy in me tries to steer me away;
    You are right, I protect you from harm.
I still hope for the best in the people I meet;
    Someday you'll wake up with alarm.

When I see selfless acts my throat gets a lump;
    You are hopeless and over the hill.
Still I too often think of myself at the first;
    And you should, don't rely on good will.

Thank you, Greed, for your care and the gift
    that you bring;
    Hold on now, don't go turning on *me.*
You are there as the yin to the yang I desire;
    I'm so glad you can see me as We.

Chapter 3

ABUNDANCE IS
AN ATTITUDE

ORTH WILLIAMSON'S daddy was serious about picking names. He could have chosen to name his new son Edward or Thomas. Both were solid names from an old family tree. But, taking his inspiration from the great retailer, J. Cash Penney, he passed on his own first name and the legacy that went with it — Worth Williamson Jr. It was to be prophetic — or maybe it was just Pygmalian — less a sign of the future than a self-fulfilling prophecy!

Worth was for several years my banker while I lived in Charlotte, North Carolina. He is the founder, CEO, and visionary leader of the

First Charlotte Bank. I was an early customer when there was only a single branch at the corner of Queens and Providence. Today, First Charlotte has five branches, each with Worth's namesake trademark — service with worth.

When I heard the wisecracking, gum-smacking center fielder played by Madonna in the film *A League of Their Own* say, "Mae's not a name, it's an attitude," I thought of Worth. The line says volumes about Worth's approach to partnering with customers. Worth is not just the tag he answers to; it's his attitude.

Worth founded the bank with customer partnership in mind. He wanted the kind of neighborly experience most customers would warmly recall from their past. Consequently, First Charlotte Bank was the only bank in town with an old-fashioned, help-yourself popcorn machine in the lobby. It was the only bank that, on rainy days, erected a canvas tunnel to connect the parking lot with the lobby. I think First Charlotte's automatic teller machines were the first in town to state "Good morning, Dr. Bell" on the instruction screen when I inserted my bank card. While most front-line bank employees in the city dressed in costumes on Halloween, First Charlotte's employees followed that practice on many other days — a bunny at Easter time, elves at Christmas. . . .

Cartoons festooned First Charlotte's drive-up windows. Drive-up tellers gave out doggy treats along with receipts to patrons with canines in their cars. The list goes on, but you get the idea. Worth gave customers worth; in turn, customers thought he was worthy of their business — all of it.

Worth has an abundance attitude. His take on life is "I have gifts to share with all who pass my way. The more I share, the more gifts I will have to share. The more gifts I share, the more people there will be that I can share with."

24

The harvest of abundance is mutual growth

Worth-style service is about mutual growth — a circular process like a snowball rolling downhill. Abundance-based customer service is not a zero-sum algebraic proposition. Native Americans did it with corn: plant the best, and the crop will grow more bountiful each year. Worth "planted" his best in customers, and all grew as a result.

We live in an era of economic ambivalence. Contemporary buying, selling, and serving are about maintaining margins on one side and finding bargains on the other. Customers want it fast, cheap — and their way. They also want it good. They are unwilling to sacrifice one attribute for another. This makes the service equation particularly challenging as cost-cutting companies carve full-time employees from payrolls. What's left is fewer to serve more, and part-timers with potentially less commitment to fighting for marketplace victories.

Against this backdrop, there is potential for conflict when an abundance attitude steps on stage. "Where is the worth in giving when taking is so crucial to survival?" some may chide. "Besides, before we can talk bounty, we need to get past survival. What can Worth teach us besides fluffy fads, clever campaigns, and manners like our mothers taught us? Our stakeholders cannot spend good feelings or deposit thank-you notes in their checking accounts." Worth knows that partnership builds loyalty, which builds retention, which builds success.

A friend of ours, Stew Leonard, runs a large grocery store in New England. He tells of a time when a customer returned to the store after buying a ninety-nine-cent quart of eggnog. "It's spoiled!" she complained. Stew recounts, "I smelled her eggnog and realized it just smelled like eggnog. The date stamp was way in the future. The carton had been opened and the eggnog could not be resold. I felt refunding her money was not the fiscally responsible action. Besides, I wanted to set an example of being frugal. When I refused to refund her money, the woman said she was never again coming back to my store."

"So," you may be saying at this point, "you win some; you lose some. That's just the nature of customer service."

Stew continues toward his punch line. "That evening as I reflected on my late-in-the-day actions, I remembered that our average customer spends close to one hundred dollars in our store about fifty weeks a year. A loyal customer stays with us ten years before moving elsewhere. My save-a-penny action had saved our store ninety-nine cents, but it cost our store fifty thousand dollars. I decided to stop being short-term smart and long-term stupid!"

26

Abundance is a focus on relationship value, not on transaction costs

*T*he worth of great customer service requires a focus, not on the transaction costs, but on the relationship value. Transaction costs are not irrelevant, but they can, if we aren't careful, become destructively dominant. Loyal customers spend more money each year they stay with you. Devoted customers become an extension of your sales and marketing efforts; their word-of-mouth accolades bring others. They help you improve by providing feedback, not as a disappointed consumer, but as an ally. Loyal customers assertively demonstrate commitment to your success.

There *are* fickle customers on the prowl for a cheap "one-night stand" they can brag about as a financial conquest. However, smart service providers seek more mature relationships with customers in whom they can invest for a long-term payback. Smart money is on retention, not acquisition; the wise enterprise counts on depth and length of relationship, not a single transaction.

Worth Williamson was clever enough to discover that popcorn, cartoons, and costumes might bring you in, but it was partnership that would bring you back. He kept tabs on my business challenges and triumphs. "How did your seminar go in New York last week?" he would remember to ask. "That article you wrote on service recovery really helped me. I made copies for all my managers." While very skilled at unearthing customer aims, he was also adept at unleashing customer affirmations.

My car battery died one day in the First Charlotte Bank parking lot — a forty-eight-month battery in its sixty-fourth month! The nearest Wal-Mart/Sears/Firestone was two miles away. I went into the bank to call for transportation to a store to buy a replacement. "Take my car," Worth said as he overheard my call in the lobby. I turned to see his hand extended, holding the keys to his station wagon. IIis gesture went way beyond the typical "Use the phone in my office if you like" offer that others consider good service. Worth is a devotee of expressions of plenty, not acts of politeness.

An abundance attitude has magnetic impact on customers. It attracts them because it conveys to the customer the kind of unconditional positive regard that characterizes relationships at their best. Customers like the way they feel when dealing with service providers who have such an orientation. They feel valued, not used. They enjoy relationships with value and substance far more than encounters that are functional but hollow.

The noncompetitive nature of effective partnership means approaching the relationship with a "Cast bread upon the water" orientation. Each contribution to the relationship causes it to grow and prosper. An abundance attitude creates a legacy of affirmation — it lives on in the language customers use to describe the service provider.

Where is First Charlotte these days? It continues to thrive. There's talk of merger and expansion. There will no doubt be more branches, more loan growth, more deposits as customers discover Worth's commitment of worth to customers. As abundance is demonstrated, it becomes infectious.

❝ No one would remember the Good Samaritan if he only had good intentions. ❞

— Margaret Thatcher

Chapter 4

SERVICE AS GIFT GIVING

I WAS BORN AND RAISED in South Georgia. People from North Georgia simply say they are from Georgia; people from the blessed part of the state, below Macon, always add the proud qualifier "South." For a long time I thought South Georgia might be a separate state from Georgia, like South Carolina and South Dakota. In some ways I guess it was, and probably still is.

Most South Georgia farmers raised cows. Most of them secured their cows in a pasture with wire fences topped by a single strand of barbed wire. And most farmers had the occasional rebellious cow or three get out of the pasture to wander up and down the highway or country road. My dad

was one of the farmers. When his cows escaped their pastures to the north, they wound up in farmer Hightower
Gilder's territory; east-pasture escapees would roam
farmer David Hartley's land.

How the two men dealt with the occasional intruder
taught me a lot about service as a gift. Hightower would
usually call us the minute he spotted my dad's white-faced
Hereford cows — seemed like always early Sunday morning. "Ray," he'd sternly say, "you got a bunch of your cows
out up here. You'd better send one of your young 'uns up
here to get 'em back in." My dad would always express
polite gratitude and dispatch one of us for the rescue mission. You could always tell that Hightower thought he was
doing us a big favor. He could, after all, simply let the cows
wander and nature take its course. Besides, they weren't
his cows; he was simply a neighbor serving a neighbor.

David was different. He'd get *his* boys up, find the
break in the fence, drive Dad's cows back to their proper
place, temporarily fix the fence, and *then* call. Now, guess
what we did when Hightower's cows roamed south? And
you can no doubt figure out who got a real special gift
when the Hartley cows strayed onto Bell land.

30

Gift giving is an attitude, not a tactic

Customers who experience gift giving become
advocates, loyal fans, and champions. Gift-
giving service fosters customer reciprocity — but without
any obligation. We telephoned Hightower every time we
spotted his cows; he expected it. But we went to bat for
David, and he *never* expected it. Hightower was a good
neighbor; he served us well. David was like a member of
the family.

When I moved to Dallas in 1992, I quickly learned
the challenges and costs of Dallas–Fort Worth Airport

parking, after a month of never being able to find a parking place. I elected to forgo the joys of driving and hire a driver to take me to and from the airport. My goal was not luxury, but convenience and time management — I could use the thirty-minute drive to make phone calls and do paperwork, and I never again worried that my flight would leave without me. I hired Matt Payesteh of M.P. Limousine, who provided lots of value-added extras: a fresh newspaper, access to his car phone when my cellular phone batteries failed me, and assistance with luggage — all the important elements of good limousine service.

Our first Christmas we spent away, traveling on holiday to visit family and friends in Georgia and North Carolina. Driving by our Dallas home over the holidays, Matt realized that our house was the only one in the neighborhood without decorations. We had left without realizing the significance of violating such an important neighborhood tradition. Without consultation, Matt went to the store, purchased and erected an outdoor tree in our front yard, complete with lights and an on-off electric timer switch. We were stunned by his thoughtfulness. The tree demonstrated gift-giving service. Matt put it up because he wanted to — with no expectation of any payback from us. Of course, it cemented our partnership!

31

Service gifts aren't golden — they're Samaritan

*A*nyone who would question the Golden Rule ("Do unto others as you would have them do unto you") has to be un-American, heathen, and callous — right? There is nothing wrong with the Golden Rule! If everyone practiced it, there would be no war, no famine, no poverty, and very little sadness in the world. Having said that, I want to look at the language of the

Golden Rule. I think it is flawed — at least as it applies to gift giving.

The concept of the Golden Rule is great. The part that bothers me is "as you would have them do unto you." This phrase has a kind of self-centered, using-"me"-as-the-criterion dimension to it. How about substituting "as they need"? Why should I use my needs as the yardstick? Instead of the Golden Rule, I prefer the "Good Samaritan" concept of gift giving. Regardless of your religious interest or preference, that biblical parable communicates the heart of gift giving.

The late Dr. Clarence Jordan was a brilliant biblical scholar and theologian who translated much of the New Testament into Southern dialect to provide a richer interpretation of the Bible. In *The Cotton Patch Version*, written at the height of the '60s era of racial tension, he translated the Good Samaritan parable as follows:

32

> A man was going from Atlanta (Jerusalem) to Albany (Jericho) and some gangsters held him up. When they had robbed him of his wallet and brand-new suit, they beat him up and drove off in his car, leaving him unconscious on the shoulder of the highway.
>
> Now it just so happened that a white preacher was going down that same highway. When he saw the fellow, he stepped on the gas and went scooting by. Shortly afterwards a white Gospel song leader came down the road, and when he saw what had happened, he too stepped on the gas.
>
> Then, a black man traveling that way came upon the fellow, and what he saw moved him to tears. He stopped and bound up his wounds as best he could, drew some water from his thermos jug to wipe away the blood and laid him on the back seat. He drove on into Albany and took him to the hospital and said to the nurse, "You all take good care of this white man I found hurt on the highway. Here's the only two dollars I got, but you all keep account of what he owes, and if he can't pay it, I'll settle up with you when I make a pay-day."

The response of the Good Samaritan was not just a random act of kindness. It was an endowment made out of a heartfelt urge to contribute. It was a gift, not a value-added gesture. It was service at its very best.

The efforts of some service providers to "go the extra mile" for customers can have the feel of bribery — they've got a bartering, quid pro quo dimension to them. The service provider indirectly says to the customer, "I have given you something special, now I expect you to respond with your allegiance." The customer is induced to feel the tug of guilt akin to the one we feel when we get a wedding or graduation invitation from someone we barely know and elect *not* to send a present.

Service as gift giving is not conditional; it is a selfless act. It is service emanating from the inner joy of service, not a tactical decision. It is service as a force, not service as a magnet. And it has a magical aspect to it. It works only when there is no expectation or requirement of a response in kind. Yet it evokes a loyalty and bond from the recipient that typically yields a response in kind. Reciprocity is the effect or result when reciprocity is not the intent or objective. David Hartley rescued our cows because that's just the way David was. However, as I think back on those many incidents, we seemed always to *want* to return his cattle in the same way.

33

So what does this mean for business? We could "gift" ourselves into bankruptcy. We'd all feel great — until the creditors started repossessing our furniture! Business, after all, is not a voluntary, charitable organization. Stakeholders don't invest in us because of our philanthropy, they invest in us because of our profit. The Red Cross or American Heart Association or Snow Hill Baptist Church might justify gift giving, but not business. The existence of a business is tied to bottom-line results, which implies clever bartering and ruthless negotiating.

Does it, really? Or have we just made up that tit-for-tat paradigm? What if an enterprise looked for ways to give to customers in an expressive, unbridled way? Not extravagant or foolish; not trash and trinkets. And not gifts that put the receiver under obligation.

What happens in other relationships when you give with "other" focus *and* casual flamboyance? How are other relationships in your life altered by beneficial gestures free of any "What's in it for me?" component?

Try something: starting today, pick a customer you like, enjoy, and are proud to have as a customer. Think about a gift you might give. Think of personal favors rather than tangible objects.

Now when you've finished planning for a favorite customer, select a customer you don't particularly like, don't enjoy, and almost wish you didn't have as a customer. Take the exact same approach that you did with the one you like. The specific gifts may be different, but the approach should be the same. After one month, examine how the relationship has changed. Examine also how you have changed and how you feel. Then decide if the "giver" orientation is more powerful than the "give to get" orientation to service. Let me know how it turns out!

34

66 *Service is the rent you pay for room on this earth.* 99
— Shirley Chisholm

Chapter 5

PASSIONATE CONNECTIONS

AROLD BOYD RETIRED in 1983 after thirty-seven years with Arkansas Power & Light Co. The editor of the *Times Dispatch* in Walnut Ridge, Arkansas, considered putting his retirement announcement in the newspaper's obituary section.

No, Harold did not pass away! "Boyd," as he is called by all who know him, is still very much alive. But with his retirement, hundreds of customers experienced the emotional loss of a partnership led by a man passionately in tune with their welfare. He won "Man of the Year" that year by a country mile. And he had to get a large trailer to take home all the gifts well-wishers brought by the office during his last week of work. People came out of the wood-work to celebrate a service provider even the late Sam Walton considered "a real special man."

At the end of *Howards End,* E. M. Forster slammed on the brakes after hundreds of energetic pages with the final words: "Only connect." At the time I read the book, the advice fell wasted on my nonchalant, "no big deal" attitude. However, years later, after several relationship challenges, I more clearly understand and more deeply appreciate Forster's simple but cogent counsel.

Connection is the essence of powerful relationships. A great partnership is analogous to an electrical circuit. The lights go out in partnerships when either of two situations occurs: a poor connection, that is, partners out of sync; or a power or energy shortage. The latter occurs more often. Both are typically avoidable and needless.

Harold Boyd was once asked the secret of his long and devoted marriage to Martha Jane. His impish smile and "aw shucks" style almost gave away the answer before his words were spoken: "We got married, but we never quit dating." One of the family's most prized photos is of Boyd and Martha Jane passionately kissing in front of the house — no doubt a sudden, unmitigated, spontane-ous expression of affection while waiting for the photog-rapher to put in a new roll of film. He gave his customers daring devotion cut from the same cloth.

Partnerships are about everlastingly enthusiastic investment. Great customer relationships never move to the "taken for granted" stage. While there is the comfort of familiarity and the ease of working-togetherness, the connection is perpetually passionate. Great partnerships exhibit courageous commitment. Partners in great part-nerships "put out" — that is, they make it a point to assert their belief in their relationship. They refuse to rely on a tacit "They know how we feel about them." No news is *not* good news; no news is *no* news! And partnerships need the affirmation of the good news of commitment as dem-onstrated through contributions to the relationship.

After a siege of bad weather that downed power lines in a part of Lawrence County, Boyd not only called the important rice farmers affected by the outage, he and his staff called every customer. But there was more. When Bubba Secoy's mother passed away after a long illness, Boyd sent flowers to the funeral. When Jim Allison's oldest boy was appointed to West Point, Boyd called Jim to congratulate him. Ruby Wilcoxson got a "just dropped by" visit one time after she had a breaker box problem repaired. And it was not just "Boyd, the neighbor" making the call; it was always "This is Boyd down at Arkansas Power."

Death by vanilla

*M*ost customer relationships do not end with a storm of sound and fury. Most partnerships do not end in a fit of dissonance or from a caustic conflict. Most customer relationships "vanilla" to death. Either or both partners so take the relationship for granted that the customer steals away in the quiet of night.

When Stew Leonard Sr. of Stew Leonard's Dairy Store suggested that service providers "love the customer," he was not positing a passive posture, he was advising an active assertion. Customers know you are committed to the partnership based only on what they experience. The affirmation of devotion is known only through energetic contribution and passionate commitment.

Customer partnerships benefit from surprising diversity. The "we never stopped dating" dimension means making an effort to provide value added based solely on commitment to the relationship. Great partners put energy into unearthing ways to endow the relationship with extra joy — for joy's sake. They pursue prizes of intrigue, given without expectation of anything in return. They believe in the sanctity of contribution.

Boyd's partnering style started even when he was a "grunt" (the person on the ground who throws tools up to the lineman on the pole). His career climb from grunt to lineman to serviceman to local manager to district manager was due largely to his committed passion for customers. Most customer contact people know their customers' names; Boyd also knew the names of their pets. When the Walnut Ridge Chamber of Commerce needed a leader people respected, they made Boyd their president. It was not so much his energy as his *directed* energy people admired. His customer convictions were always punctuated with exclamation points.

"Service is typically lousy today," says Larry Hollar, executive vice president of Fairfield Chair in Lenoir, North Carolina, "not because people don't care about service. It's because they don't care about the customer." Too often service providers confuse customer service with warranties, service guarantees, service contracts, and all manner of high-sounding procedural pap.

Service is the flesh-and-blood, mushy, non-quantifiable, heartfelt manifestation of devotion to people who look to us for assistance in meeting a need. If the service provider does not like the customer, the customer will know it. And the customer will either go elsewhere or keep the relationship as superficial as her investment is shallow. Stated differently, the customer's economic investment in the service provider is too often directly tied to the service provider's emotional investment in the customer.

Implied invitations for customer energy

John Longstreet is the general manager of the Harvey Hotel in Plano, Texas. His 1993 Christmas card contained not only a handwritten note expressing his gratitude for my patronage, but also a donation flyer and a note about his favorite charity. What a connection! It was as if he were saying, "This is something I am passionate about and I wanted to share it with my partners."

Boyd also had his passionate connections with customers. As a manager long since promoted beyond the ranks of line operator, he once "burned" a pole while helping out a short-handed crew and wound up first in the hospital, then convalescing at home. "Burning" (a.k.a. "cutting out") is utility-industry jargon for falling from a power pole while trying to grip the pole you are straddling. Once you begin to fall, according to Boyd, you have two options: either break your back on impact or wind up with a body full of splinters from hugging the wooden pole all the way down. Boyd opted to hug wood!

Boyd's number-one concern while being wheeled into the emergency room was his connection with customers. He first demanded that all his office calls be forwarded to his hospital room. By the time he was convalescing at home, his loyal customers were simply bypassing the office and calling Boyd at home. Their practice stuck, much to Boyd's delight. Right up until he retired, when customers were unable to reach Boyd at the office they just called him at home. For several months after he retired, some called him when they had a need to reach Arkansas Power.

Partnership connections are solid and without reserve. Great partners are not doubtful duos; they connect with the dynamic of unbridled devotion. The super power in the partnership is the charge each gets from contributing to the other's prosperity. Partners in such relationships are as committed to the other's success and joy as to their own — often more committed. Partnerships energize; each partner is ignited and energized by the experience of partnering.

Boyd-like passion for customers is a vital building block in enlisting their loyalty. Customers become devoted to service providers who are devoted to them — even more devoted than the grocer who, while selling you two loaves of bread, gives you a fresh-baked cookie to "take home to little Lorine." Value added helps, but the memorable connections are those grounded in fulfilling needs in devoted and dedicated ways. Passionate connections leave the customer feeling celebrated by the experience.

Dr. Robert Peterson is a professor at The University of Texas who has thoroughly studied the tenets of customer loyalty. His studies repeatedly show that customers with feelings at the extreme positive end of the emotional continuum are those most loyal. Satisfied customers take you for granted; but those who tell love stories about you (as in, "I just love shopping at...") are devoted fans and lifelong customers. Partners are patrons of passionate connections who never tire of donations of devotion. Like Harold Boyd, they retire with a smile and a legacy of enthusiastically delivered contributions.

40

"Life is either a daring adventure or nothing."
— Helen Keller

Chapter 6

SERVING IN THE DARK

I WAS DAZZLED year before last — absolutely stunned! — by an extraordinary service experience. The service came from someone I have never seen; it happened "in the dark." Yet I now have a partnership with this distinguished service provider.

I flew from my office to Portland, Maine, then drove to Lewiston to work with a health-care client. Somewhere along that three-hour, two-stop flight and the forty-five-minute rental-car drive, I misplaced five slides I needed for a keynote speech some thirty-six hours later in Orlando, Florida. A check through the yellow pages and a few late calls from Lewiston to audiovisual shops in Portland led me to the answering machine of Caribou Visual Presentations. During the lengthy but friendly recording, a fax number was mentioned. I began to plot how I might get new slides in my short time frame.

Very early the following morning before leaving my Lewiston hotel, I faxed a handwritten plea, a copy of my calling card, and a draft of my simple but much-needed slides to the Caribou fax number. "A shot in the dark," I thought. My hope was that Caribou would sense my desperation, produce the slides in record time, and deliver them to the car-rental return desk at the Portland airport as I rushed through to catch my 2:00 p.m. flight to Orlando. I also expected them to send me a handsome bill for this "beyond the call of duty" request.

Midmorning, from the office of the Lewiston client, I called to determine whether Caribou had received my faxed note. I was disappointed to find that their answering machine was still on as it had been the previous evening. I repeated my predicament and need. At noon, another quick call yielded the same recording. I left Lewiston for the Portland airport and turned in my rental car without bothering to ask if there had been a message left. On my Portland-D.C.-Orlando flight, I planned how I would present my speech at nine o'clock the following morning *without* slides.

The speech went fine, and I chalked up my episode with the phantom Caribou as a gallant yet acknowledged long shot that simply failed to pan out. However, when I checked with my answering service after my Orlando speech, I had received an apologetic message from the owner of Caribou, indicating that he was out of town on a family emergency and was unable to respond to my request. As it turned out, he *had* left a message for me at the airport rental-car desk. A week later, dazzlement happened! I received the following letter:

Dear Chip:

I'm very sorry we could not connect in time to help
you out when you were up in Lewiston last week. I
was down in New Jersey on a family matter when I
checked in with my machine and got your message.
I called the Ramada in Lewiston but they told me
you had already checked out. I then called the Hertz
desk at the Portland airport — the woman at the desk
said you were due to return your rental car later that
afternoon. So I left a message with her explaining
my situation and giving her the name of my competition in the hope that he could help you out (though
I knew by that time it would probably be too late).

I would like to thank you for considering Caribou
Visual Presentations — your request could have been
handled easily had I not been called away. I realize
that your slides have probably been found or reshot
by this point, but I offer you the enclosed slides in
appreciation of your consideration. Best of luck in
future seminars!

Yours truly,

Richard Vaglia

Inside his letter was a set of gorgeous slides! I
immediately called Caribou and left a message on the now-
familiar answering machine indicating that I was very
pleased and expected an invoice. Later that same day, my
answering service took the message from Caribou:
"Thanks for considering us. The slides are our gift to you."
Now, I will tell you, folks, I would not even *consider* getting future slides from anyone other than Caribou, even
though they are nine states away. We are now partners.

We are in the middle of two major trends that make
my awesome experience both timely and relevant: service quality and service convenience. First, the service era
is making customers more assertive in their service

requirements and much tougher with the grades they put on their "Did I get good service?" report cards. Second, customers are requiring that service be provided in ways that are increasingly convenient and efficient (e.g., post office to overnight mail to fax to who knows what next). These two trends will result in more "serving in the dark." But how do you create a partnership with a customer whose face you never see? Does partnership require a face-to-face encounter? How do you create a positive bond with a customer whose voice you never hear?

There have always been a host of service providers whose only service signature was the quality of the work they left for the customer — the hotel housekeeper, the auto repair person on the other side of the Customers Not Allowed Beyond This Point sign, the janitor on the graveyard shift, the night nurse who checks your medical stats after major surgery when you are too drugged to communicate. But what about service providers who depend on a strong interpersonal relationship with the customer for repeat business? With the advent of modems, faxes, and answering machines, there will be a growing number of Caribous partnering "in the dark."

The route to creating a positive service relationship with customers requiring service without direct contact is to simulate the quality of a partnership. As with service in general, effective management of service details can turn an "at arm's length" encounter into a responsive kinship experience. It means first making the relationship matter, then seeking subtle but powerful actions designed to communicate care, concern, and authenticity.

44

Personalize routine correspondence

*C*ustomers have come to expect a certain amount of form-letter communicating. The service greats, however, take "form" one step beyond.

Marriott Hotel customers rave about getting a "letter from Bill" in response to their completing the Marriott "Will You Let Me Know?" comment card. The kudos are not about the real ink of Bill's signature, but the tailored language that makes the letter read as though it were individually composed.

I use a service for refurbishing my laser-printer cartridges. When the Toner Low signal flashes on my printer, I pull the cartridge, mail it to Toner Service Inc. in St. Louis, and within forty-eight hours get a refurbished cartridge for about half the cost of a brand-new cartridge. A personalized form letter accompanies the returned laser cartridge. One letter I received (at Super Bowl season) contained a handwritten P.S.: "I'll bet you are real proud of the Cowboys about now!" The clerk or packer or someone noticed my Texas address and scrawled a little "value added" to the letter. I felt as though I had heard from a friend!

Create back-door access

*R*emember growing up in the neighborhood? Strangers came in through the front door, but real friends came in the back. Not only was it generally easier, it typically put you more quickly in the heart of the home — the kitchen and the den.

Access is always important in a good service-delivery system. With "serving in the dark," it is important for the customer to perceive easy access to the service provider. While physical access may not always be relevant, psychological access clearly is. Armed with fax numbers and twenty-four-hour answering services, customers want to know they can order "in the dark" service whenever they need it.

L. L. Bean, Spiegel, Land's End, and other premier catalog sales companies have made their mark in part because of easy access. I picked Caribou because they were the only video presentations company in Portland that referenced a fax number on their after-hours answering machine. I was able to fax my note and slides draft from the hotel before leaving for a breakfast meeting with the client. The organizations that succeed in this service-sensitive era will be those that invite the customer to access them any time, in many ways, and with ease.

Look for patterns and find clues to tailor responses

46

*T*he customer-service representative at my bank, someone I have neither seen nor talked with by phone, had been watching the flow of money through my business checking account. Making a few calculations, she determined that a different type of checking account would provide me a better return. She dropped a note and brochure in the mail, including a signature card to open the account. I switched accounts based solely on her attentiveness to my needs, plus her personalized response.

My partner, Ron, tells stories about his housekeeper. The Zemkes rarely see her, but through notes and customized gifts, he and his wife think of the housekeeper as a member of their family. Since the Zemkes are Italian-food buffs, the housekeeper keeps an eye on their food stock and occasionally replaces an "off the beaten path" item that the housekeeper is more likely to spot than the "chef."

Encourage customer candor

*C*andor is a key attribute of any effective partnership, whether it's with a spouse, best
friend, or customer. Since the distant service provider is
devoid of face-to-face (and often ear-to-ear) exchange with
customers, "serving in the dark" has a special requirement for the extraordinary pursuit of candor. That relent-
less hunt for honesty takes cleverness, persistence, and
responsiveness to what is learned.

The Plaza Club, an upscale concierge level atop
the Radisson Mark Plaza hotel in Alexandria, Virginia,
not only positions the comment card in conspicuous (and
rotating) locations in the guest's room, but has the guest's
name and address already written (in longhand) on the
comment card. The guest naturally thinks, "Since they
have already gone to this much trouble to partially fill in
the card, the least I can do is complete it." The Plaza Club
manager reports that the return rate is unusually high.

Bob Hill Lawn Care takes care of our lawn. Bob
has a key to the backyard gate and garage, and leaves his
bill in the mailbox. Our lawn is cut, sprayed, seeded, aer-
ated, and fertilized while we are at work. Bob's main contact with us is through his monthly invoice, which he has
wisely turned into a comment card. "I am pleased with
how your grass is looking and I hope you are," one invoice
left for me said recently. "You probably noticed I moved
that old azalea to a sunnier spot. Dr. Bell, you can help
me a lot by letting me know what you think." No "file 13"
for that comment section; I complete it in detail!

"Serving in the dark" does not have to be silent
service, stoically given without customer rapport. The
superior service provider finds ways to build a partner-

47

ship with distant customers even if that relationship must be more that of a dedicated pen pal than a friendly neighbor. As customers require better service delivered more quickly and with greater convenience, "serving in the dark" will become, to paraphrase the familiar ad line, "the next-best substitute to actually being there."

66 *I expect to pass through this world but once. Any good therefore that I can do, or any kindness that I can show to any fellow creature, let me do it now. Let me not defer or neglect it, for I shall not pass this way again.* 99

— Stephen Grellet

TRUST

trust *n.* 1. A reliance on the integrity, strength, ability, or justice of another person or thing; faith; reliance. 2. Confident expectation, anticipation, or hope.

Faith, Hope, and Partnership

I stood with a crowd in the mall,
intrigued by a gallery wall.
  The art was unique,
  with secrets to seek.
"Stereo graphic," they're called.

At first they appeared quite a bore,
just colors and shapes, nothing more.
  But the man next to me
  cried, "Look, it's a tree."
He excitedly moved to explore.

Then more people saw hidden art,
And all acted suddenly smart.
  "I need some advice,
  my eyes won't suffice."
I plead with the merchant, "Have heart."

"Look deep in the picture, let go,
have faith that the secrets will show,
  keep focus ahead,
  assume you'll be led
to richer dimensions below."

The hope from this merchant's wise thought
provided the insight I sought.
  But more than this art,
  I realized I'm part
of a "mono graphic" I'd fought.

I vowed to pursue a new door,
to find deeper meaning, the core.
His advice served me true,
as I sought to renew
relationships needing much more.

This odd artwork paralleled truth:
great partnerships do not need proof.
They only need trust,
bold faith is a must,
and real depth will not stay aloof.

"Look deep in your partners, let go,
have faith that the secrets will show,
keep focus ahead,
assume you'll be led
to richer dimensions below."

Chapter 7

IN CUSTOMERS WE TRUST

EVER TRIED TO ARRANGE to have a complimentary dinner delivered on credit to someone in another state? The experience starts with a long-distance call and ends with "Sorry, we don't take credit cards" and lots of disappointment. You are left wishing L. L. Bean, Land's End, and J. Crew all had food divisions and delivered!

But I'm ahead of myself. It had been a dreary January week for my Minneapolis partner. The post-holiday blues had collided with his year-end paperwork to leave him with a less-than-cheery disposition. "Why not treat him and his wife to a 'top of the line' pizza (he loves pizza), delivered when and how he wants it?" I thought, still basking in the seasonal spirit of giving — and the more forgiving Texas climate.

I telephoned Minneapolis information. With a little prodding, the directory-assistance operator was able to come up with a list of restaurants in my partner's suburban, bordering-on-rural neighborhood. I called the first, started my story, and was quickly treated to a terse, "Naw, we don't deliver." As I listened to the premature dial tone, I found myself thinking, "I never even got to tell him the 'and I'll pay you $100,000 to deliver it' part!" Two food establishments later, the no-delivery refrain had changed tunes to "Sorry, that's outside our delivery range." Three establishments after that, I was getting "Great idea — but we don't take credit cards." My Good Samaritan gesture was starting to become very expensive, with seven Texas-to-Minnesota phone calls and still no pizza delivery possible. Then I reached Ben James at Gina Maria's in Excelsior — and my belief in the spirit of service was quickly renewed.

Ben patiently listened to my goal and my long string of disappointing long-distance encounters. "You're calling from Texas?" he asked almost in disbelief. "Well," he said with resignation in his voice, "we don't take credit cards either — but I trust you. You just give me your order, I'll call your partner to arrange for a convenient delivery time, and you can just mail me a check." And — this is the best part — Ben even called me back ten minutes later (long distance on *his* nickel) to let me know that he had tried my partner's phone number, gotten no answer, and would continue trying. "He may have to get his pizza tomorrow night, but I won't let you down," he said with a big smile in his voice.

I sat back relieved — and a little in awe. I was moved by the whole experience. What had made this encounter so special? What was it that made me gladly say, "Ben, you've been so helpful I will be adding a 20 percent tip to your check. Would you mail me your menu so I can use your services again?"? It was not his responsiveness, his warmth, or even his understanding, though they helped. My feeling of being served above and beyond was bound up in his friendly assertion, "but I trust you." At the core of partnership is trust.

Whoa! I can already hear the objections, the stern whispers of caution from the auditors, building to a shout. The doubting-Thomas brigade are loading their bottom-line guns for an attack on this naive romantic stuck in yesteryear — so it seems — when doors were left unlocked and your word was your bond. "We have a new era of sabotage, selfishness, and cynicism," they caustically assert. "If all our employees acted like Ben, we would be belly up before next Wednesday."

Is the world that mean and cross a place? It makes me wonder just how many — if any — businesses have gone under because they regularly demonstrated their superior service in part by trusting customers. Sure, one-tenth of one percent of customers truly are evil and get their jollies or impress their friends by ripping off businesses. But if companies concentrate on protecting themselves from a small, unsavory part of the population, what message are they sending to the greater customer population?

A highly successful Charlotte-based cafeteria-style deli restaurant called Arthur's locates the cash register on the opposite side of the building from the serving line. Patrons enter, order over the counter, get their food, eat, then pay on their way out. There is no check; you simply tell the cashier what you ate and pay for it. "Don't you worry about people cheating you?" I asked the owner one day. "Not really," he said. "We know a few do; we see them. But what we lose in shrinkage, we more than make up in regular customers who come here *because* they like to be trusted." His proof is the twenty-minute wait it takes just to get into this place at lunch every day!

What is it about trust that makes customers feel valued? In part, it communicates that one-half of a partnership is reaching out to the other half. And customers reward partnerships. The smart money is on customer retention — turning service samplers into long-term partners. Not only is it much more expensive to acquire a customer than to keep one (about five to one), but the average customer, in year five of his relationship with you, will spend considerably more than he did in year one or two or three.

Customers who are trusted tend to become ex officio members of your sales-and-marketing department. Stanley Marcus, founder of Neiman-Marcus in Dallas, enjoys telling the story of the young debutante who returned a $175 evening gown after one evening's rough treatment and wanted her money back. "It was obvious her own reckless behavior had left the dress in shambles. But I gave her back her money. And in 1935, one hundred seventy-five dollars was a lot of money for a dress." Marcus beams as he relates the punch line: "But not only did she spend over a hundred thousand with me over the next thirty years, she made sure all her wealthy friends did likewise. Trusting her turned out to be a great investment!"

The January 1994 issue of *Success* magazine reported on Santa Clara, California-based McAfee Associates, one of the world's leading antiviral software companies. McAfee's success is tied in part to its practice of allowing customers to download McAfee software programs from an electronic bulletin board. The announcement at the beginning of each program encourages users to mail in a payment if they elect to keep the software. "We depend on our customers' honesty," says president John McAfee. The "We trust you" shareware approach has paid off handsomely: revenues of $6.9 million in 1991 tripled by year-end '93. According to the *Success* article, their programs are used by two-thirds of the *Fortune* 100 companies. And their opinion on customers who rip them off? "Freeloaders are unofficial salespeople," reports John. "Trust makes American business work."

The waiters and waitresses at Vincenzo's Ristorante in Omaha, Nebraska, greet patrons at their table with a pitcher of "honor wine" — an excellent Chianti. "Enjoy this if you like," one waitress said to us recently. "We charge by the glass. At the end of the meal, just let me know how many glasses you had and I will add it to your bill." When I asked the owner on our way out how many patrons drink the Chianti, he smiled and said, "Most — it's one of our best features!"

So why doesn't every service provider think and act like Gina Maria's, Arthur's, McAfee, Vincenzo's, and Stanley Marcus? It starts with short-term thinking that measures the encounter cost to the penny but fails to consider the worth of the relationship. It is often grounded in a controlling, Scrooge-like management philosophy that says, "Give 'em an inch and they'll take a mile. If we didn't have tough rules and plenty of controls, if the customers didn't scalp us, our employees would."

What would I do if it were my store? I'd declare a sixty-day trust period. I would encourage my employees to demonstrate more trust to customers. I'd ask employees to identify areas where "We don't trust you" messages are telegraphed to customers. Then I'd separate out those areas where legal or quasi-legal issues prevent altering practice.

With the areas left, I would outline new "trusting" steps for employees to take. And I'd work hard to remember that to get employees to trust customers, they must see that I trust them. At the end of the sixty-day period, I would briefly interview a few regular customers to get their reactions.

How can you demonstrate trust to customers? Here are a couple of quick ideas to get you rolling:

Consider a service guarantee. Make the guarantee for a part of your service that could have an easy-to-explain guarantee. Service guarantees need to be devoid of fine print, simple to administer (no tedious forms), and easy for the customer to collect on (no "We'll mail you a check in ninety days"). Service guarantees might be as simple as "We promise that you will be happy with our service, or your dessert is on us" or "Repairs completed within twenty-four hours and to your satisfaction, or we pay the tab." Pilot the service guarantee for a limited time, or for a portion of your business, and see what you learn. Remember that customer and employee feedback needs to be a key part of your assessment.

Hampton Inn's "100 percent satisfaction guarantee" states that if you are not completely satisfied, "we don't expect you to pay." Hampton's research has shown that 99 percent of the guests who invoked their guarantee would stay at a Hampton Inn again based on the attitude of the hotel staff when they requested or received compensation under the hotel's guarantee.

Trust employees more. Trusting customers starts with trusting employees — especially since employees are customers as well. Examine your internal rules and procedures to isolate those that have a "guilty until proven innocent" theme or tone. Rewrite or weed out the ones that apply to all in order to catch the few. Take a look at places where the leading theme is "Prove it to me first" and find ways to send a more trusting message. Bill Lee, CEO of Charlotte-based Duke Power Company, is fond of saying to employees, "Ask why, and if the answer to the question is not compelling, do what you think is right, and it probably will be."

The magical power of trust is that it begets trust. If you demonstrate trust to customers, they will trust you back. Such trust shapes their perception of you as a service provider. Trusted customers will be more tolerant, more patient, and more forgiving when mistakes occur, even defending you to other customers ("Oh, this is not their normal way of performing; this is an exception"). They will also perceive higher quality and greater value for their service dollar.

Today's customers are in search of quality. Their demands for service that is great are increasingly taking priority over "I simply want the cheapest." They will reward with their repeat business those service providers who treat them with respect, with responsiveness, and most of all, with trust. There is no sweeter sound to a customer than "but I trust you."

"*Faith is not belief without proof, but trust without reservations.*"

— Elton Trueblood

Chapter 8

BLESSED ASSURANCE

HOWARD PERDUE was the owner, manager, and spiritual leader of the Ford Tractor dealership in McRae, Georgia, during the '50s and '60s. In that region, 185 percent of the population — practically every man, woman, child, dog, horse, and mule — was involved in the overtime occupation of worrying about soybean prices and praying for rain. Since no one could do much serious farming without a tractor and the proper plows, Mr. Perdue was the center of the universe. He was also my mother's brother.

The Perdue-farmer relationship was a special one. Few farmers started the planting season with enough money to fund all their farm implement or equipment needs. They typically bet — along with Howard — on the success of their harvest. Their new tiller, combine, or fertilizer spreader was bought on credit and a promise to pay "when I make my crop." Frequently, farmers had to literally "bet the farm" when an unexpected equipment failure led to a major unexpected expense. But the risk was not only on the customer's side.

My brother, sister, and I would occasionally play among the new tractors in Howard's showroom or chase each other down long aisles of equipment parts. We thought Uncle Howard was a rich man. After all, he owned all this neat stuff! We had no concept of how his livelihood was tied to his customers'. If their crops failed, he lost.

Howard's brand of partnership has come to remind me of an old hymn, "Blessed Assurance." One verse of that song, while clearly intending a religious message, implies powerful instructions for customer partnership. The verse goes: "Perfect submission, perfect delight, visions of rapture now burst on my sight; watching and waiting, looking above; echoes of mercy, whispers of love."

Partnerships are promises made, promises kept

*T*he Howard Perdue approach to partnership started with a covenant. He would deliver an expensive tractor to a farmer, demonstrating his faith in the customer's ability to "grow" tractor payments. But the farmer had his side of the covenant, too. While "watching and waiting" and "looking above," he (they were all "he") relied on the mercy of Howard, the loan holder. If the farmer needed more time to pay, when "we ain't had a drop in weeks," Howard almost always acceded to their wishes. The covenant also contained an unspoken assumption that if all parties were "raptured" by a bumper crop, the farmer would pay it out early.

All customer partnerships depend on blessed assurance. Assurance begets certainty; it means a guaranty both pledged with conviction and accepted with courage. It is a notice of a mutual leap of faith. It is the "I do" end of the "and thereto I plight thee my troth" promise. Howard's modus operandi communicated his belief that "we're in this together."

Professor Leonard Berry of Texas A&M University is one of the country's leading authorities on service quality. He and his colleagues have conducted countless studies on what customers value in service quality. Their findings: Customers consider empathy, confidence (he calls it assurance), responsiveness, and tangibles key service-quality factors. But the most important attribute to customers of any business is *reliability*. The quickest path to customers' ire is to make or imply a promise and fail to keep it. Howard Perdue could have taught Dr. Berry (and all of us) about the core meaning of reliability.

However, in a partnership, promises must be made in order for promises to be kept. Partnerships are not successful on a "cash and carry only" basis. They require acts of courage. The "living trust" dimension demands actions that give customers an opportunity to demonstrate "perfect submission."

"The quality of mercy is not strained," said Portia in Shakespeare's *Merchant of Venice;*

> It droppeth as the gentle rain from heaven
> Upon the place beneath. It is twice blest;
> It blesseth him that gives and him that takes.
> 'Tis mightiest in the mightiest. . . .

Howard and Portia thought a lot alike.

Parts manager Carl Vardeman, like Howard — perhaps because of him — was more than willing to come down on the empathy side of a hard-luck saga. I once heard him tell an embarrassed farmer who was pleading his cash-shortage problem, "I'm sure Mr. Perdue will under-stand your situation. He's back in the garage with Jim. I'll go and get him." I carefully watched from behind the parts counter as Howard emerged from the garage, wip-ing black engine grease from his hand. The farmer and Howard greeted each other without shaking hands (farm-ers generally only shook with the preacher when leaving the church after a good fire-and-brimstone sermon). "How's Mary?" Howard asked, attempting to alter the straight lines on the farmer's despondent face.

I didn't hear the rest of the conversation; they went behind closed doors. Mercy giving was always a private affair in those days. But when they emerged, Howard announced to Carl that Mr. Garrison would be getting a new carburetor. It was clearly a coded communication — "echoes of mercy" — a signal from Howard to Carl that credit had been extended, boundaries had been expanded, and trust had been restored. Mercy is marvelous magic! And there was no parting expression of humility from the farmer. Submission had been perfect — mutual.

Great partners are devoted fans

I was always surprised by how much Howard seemed to know about his customers. Sure, he had an economic stake in their welfare. But it was more than that. He knew, for instance, that Elmer Peavy made scrimshaw knives, that Daniel Yawn was a crack-erjack fly fisherman, that Lewis Rountree's oldest son was a highly decorated Air Force major. These were facts and fables not gleaned from barbershop talk, the men's Bible class at First Baptist, or the social page of the *Telfair Enterprise*. This was knowledge that required precision probing, dramatic listening, and lavish understanding.

Partners not only seek to learn about their partners, they look for ways to use that knowledge to give the other party public bragging opportunities. Howard did that better than almost anyone I know. And the larger the audience standing around the tractor showroom, the more assertively he'd ask, "Lewis, is your boy running the Pentagon yet?" Of course, Mr. Rountree would light up the place after such an invitation to play to his favorite topic. And Howard would fire off another "Let me pique the curiosity of anyone within earshot" question. The farmers' eavesdropping would soon turn into pumping Lewis for more information. Lewis would emerge as a local hero. Lewis probably plowed his fields more confidently after those encounters!

Part of this ritual was based on sincere curiosity. Howard really *was* interested in the status of Major Rountree. But the larger focus of this ritual seemed to be an act of devotion and admiration that cemented the partnership. This equation encompassed more than economics; it also contained "whispers of love" and "perfect delight."

65

Howard has long since retired to a leisurely life of fishing, traveling the North Carolina mountains with his wife, Ouida, and telling stories about his famous history professor daughter, Theda. The tractor store is now some other sort of small-town business. Mr. Peavy's eyesight caused him to put up his special knives, Mr. Yawn's arthritis put a halt to his fly-fishing, and Mr. Rountree now plows more heavenly pastures.

When I return for visits, I sometimes drive by the old tractor store. Waves of nostalgia take me back to a time when business was almost all about belief in the better side of enterprise. Relationships seemed more revered, partnerships more particular. Local customers were "for life" deals, like marriages. And even the "just passing through town" customers were treated like neighbors.

Howard Perdue recently celebrated his eighty-fifth birthday. Countless old partners were there watching and waiting to help celebrate the master partner. I was not there. But I heard it was a long afternoon of nostalgia overload. And all who attended left having been blessedly assured and twice blest.

66

66 *To give real service you must add something which cannot be bought or measured with money, and that is sincerity and integrity.* **99**

— Donald A. Adams

Chapter 9

LEAPS OF FAITH

RON ZEMKE AND I have enjoyed a long and productive relationship with Susan and Fred Salenger, the owners and managers of Salenger Films, a very successful training film distributor/producer headquartered in Santa Monica, California. When we negotiated our first film contract, we sat down over dinner and agreed on how we would work together.

After a simple handshake, Ron and I conceptualized, helped write, and hosted a major training film that Salenger Films produced and currently markets. There was and never has been any written contract! When the need to reshoot a part of the film lengthened the production schedule,

Fred called and offered to increase our royalty to make up for it. Where do you think we went with our next film idea?

I have learned that the Salengers deal with most of their partners without carefully crafted contracts. I have also told the Salenger story to service providers who have been surprised — no, amazed — at the impact their leaps of faith have on the quality of their partnerships with customers.

"Leap of faith" is an expression that in antiquity meant "trust without reason" — an action in which the consequences are unknown. The expressions "leap in the dark" and "blind faith" were derived from this concept of irrational hope.

A leap is far more than a hop

*P*artners do not take "hops of faith" or "jumps of faith." "Leaps" implies lunging or soaring beyond what is required to make it to the other side. There is a sort of "throw caution to the wind," reckless abandon in leaping partnerships. Hops suggest timidity; jumps are calculated to be adequate or sufficient; partnership faith is without restraint or bridle. Partners do not measure or dole out their belief in the relationship; they trust, not by the spoonful, but by the handful! They *trust,* or they don't.

Delbert Litchfield is a seawall/boathouse builder on Cedar Creek Lake in East Texas. The month after my wife and I purchased a weekend lake house near Gun Barrel, we asked different people in the area to recommend a good builder to construct a large boathouse. It seemed that Delbert was clearly the neighborhood boathouse builder of choice. So we summoned Delbert.

He arrived the same day we inquired about a bid. We spent an hour or so going over the details — a seventy-five-foot ramp, an electric boat lift, a side platform for diving and swimming, extra electrical outlets, spotlights, and so forth. He took lots of notes and drew rough diagrams. Then he did all his calculations, including his profit, in clear view, leaning over the hood of his truck. He finished and rather proudly announced, "Ten thousand on the nose!" What was actually showing in the tiny window of his calculator was "10,236.85."

"Do you need prepayment? Or a deposit?" I asked this weather-worn stranger, fully expecting the contract part of the conversation to crank up. "Naw," he drawled, "Not until you tell me you're happy with it. Besides, I know where I can find you!" He half grinned, winked, and turned off his calculator. We agreed he would begin work in a week, to finish in three. "Do you need anything?" I asked, still waiting for some catch in this "You don't know me from Adam" leap he was taking. "Yep, two things," he replied, still amused at my citified caution. "Take care of the paperwork with the Cedar Creek Lake Conservation Office — they're gonna want a fifty-dollar check — and pray for sunny weather!" I almost missed the last part as he drove into the Texas sunset.

Faith holders are lighter partners

*F*aith is a fascinating factor. It says as much about the holder as it does about the receiver. I have noticed that faith holders seem happier — or maybe lighter. They don't seem to waste energy carrying around a lot of worry about coming up short tomorrow or fretting over what might have been yesterday. The grounding for their relationships seems to come from a way-down-deep creed that harbors confidence in the character of others.

Solid partners look at relationships as repositories of fidelity, and their goal in life is to put more in them than others might offer. The way they look at it is this:

someone has to make the "trust goal" in the relationship, and they consider themselves uniquely qualified to take it over the top.

Faith holders take charge of relationships with a type of enthusiasm that is free of the governors of reason or shelters of rationality. The disappointment of occasionally being snookered seems to pale in comparison with the delight of being often surprised by the humanity that can be unleashed by simple acts of trust.

Faith holders are more than plain optimists. Optimistic people take "hops of faith." But faith holders believe in a vision of partners at their very best. Faith holders' faith springs from their undying belief in the best in themselves. It is the best in one seeking linkage with the best in another.

The Salengers could have been satisfied with a no-written-contract, handshake deal. But they raised the stakes by increasing our royalties — on their own volition. Partners assert their faith in the relationship. Faith holders play high-stakes relationships with hearts marked by trust.

So where do all these leaps of faith take us? They take us from having customers who simply come back, to having customers who loyally come back, to having customers who fervently advocate, champion, and rave to all who will listen. How many of your customers would give their best friends gift certificates to sample your services? How many would bring colleagues to witness their special relationship with you?

You may at this point be thinking, "This all sounds wonderful, and perhaps even doable, for small, mom-and-pop enterprises. But such customer faith would never fly in light of the financial factors in our organization." If you need proof, field test the idea in a limited area. It may also be helpful to remember that L. L. Bean's success is tied to faith in customers.

When a customer has a problem with one of its laptop computers, Austin-based Dell Computer sends the

70

customer a replacement, a software program to move files from the old to the new computer, and mailing labels to send in the defective computer. How many organizations would manage the return process the other way: "First, send us the defective computer. . . ."? Faith comes in various forms, some larger than others. The winners are fast becoming the ones who bet on the partnership and take leaps instead of hops.

Where do my partners and I stand with the Salengers and Ol' Delbert? For starters, we are in the middle of a discussion with the Salengers on a new film project. Delbert last summer built a two-hundred-foot section of seawall around a portion of our lake property. And he is in the middle of completing another fifty-foot section.

We are loyal fans of the Salengers and Delberts of the world. Sometimes they seem to be almost extinct. At other times it seems their numbers are growing. Perhaps the count has less to do with them than with how full of faith we choose to feel at the time. What if we all decided to act faith-full?

66 *The reason why birds can fly and we can't is simply that birds have perfect faith, for to have faith is to have wings.* 99
— J. M. Barrie, *The Little White Bird*

DREAMS

dream *n.* 1. A wild fancy or hope.
2. An aspiration; ambition.
3. Anything extremely beautiful,
fine, or pleasant. *v.* 1. To conceive
of; imagine.

Why "Customer" Begins with a "C"

There once was a land with a climate of peace
  where merchant saw patron as friend;
a promise was typically made with commitment —
  the people he served were like kin.

The words in this land were chosen with care
  to communicate meaning to others;
instead of the grammar rules guiding their thoughts,
  the sounds and the letters were brothers.

A dog was a "bark" and a ewe was a "baa,"
  the name for a cow was a "moo moo";
the label said more about message than noun;
  an auto was named a "ru-do-do."

Relationships thrived in this quaint little land
  since people saw others as allies;
"ustomer service" meant "by us" and "for us,"
  the label meant "See things through our eyes."

All ustomers showed they were loyal and true —
  they returned with their friends and their funds;
ustomers helped with their comments and thoughts
  and merchants kept hitting home runs.

One cold weary night a dark spirit came through,
  its essence brought "gimme" and greed;
the ustomers soon became surly and cross,
  the merchants used tricks to succeed.

Soon each was suspicious of everyone else,
  the spirit acquired a new name:
cash-register sounds were foremost in mind,
  so they called the dark essence "Ka chang."

Ka chang took the lead on all purchases made,
  Ka chang was in charge of all costs;
Ka chang made the merchants seem evil and mean,
  the ustomers equally lost.

Merchants were cursing the people they served,
  those patrons once treated with trust;
their cursing all led to a new name they coined:
  "customer — one who is cussed."

Then one shiny day a bold grocer declined
  to let "taking" rule out over gift;
when customers asked for twelve apples she gave
  them an extra one, simply for lift.

Soon other folks came to her store with their coins —
  they had heard of this merchant's new way;
they heard that she treated them all with respect,
  and for this they'd be happy to pay!

The word of this merchant's new style made the rounds,
  how customers shopped there with joy;
some called it a sham, just a trick, not for real;
  some said, a magnificent ploy.

Success helped a few try some similar ways
  and their customers favored them too;
soon more were resisting the style of Ka chang
  and their businesses flourished and grew.

One day in this quaint little land of weird words
  the mayor pronounced a new cause;
customers now would no longer be cursed
  and their name would go back as it was.

The ustomers now had a new lease on life
 since partnership served as their guide;
sharing felt far more fulfilling than greed —
 "ustomer" now meant "our pride."

Ka chang had moved on to another abode
 to make patrons act greedy and fuss;
the name of the buyer that's used in these lands
 still stands more for "cuss" than for "us."

Chapter 10

PARTNERING ON PURPOSE

ONE OF MY CHORES as a young boy on the farm was occasionally to move a herd of cows from one pasture to another after they had grazed all the grass to nubs. Moving a couple of hundred cows carried a special challenge. I had to keep one eye on the cows immediately in front of me, or else one of the fiestier steers would double back and I would lose a lot of time getting him back with the herd. However, if I focused all my attention on the cows immediately in front of me, I would move the herd in the wrong direction and completely miss the gate in the distance.

Essential to any effective alliance, coalition, or partnership is shared vision — mutual dream making. Partners need a clear-eyed view of the "distant gate." On the wall of a church in Sussex, England, is the 1730 inscription, "A vision without a task is but a dream; a task without a vision is drudgery; but a vision and a task are the hope of the world." Wise providers learn that the success of their customer partnerships lies in the degree to which a shared vision is mutually understood and collectively honored.

Ask a dozen partners in successful partnerships the primary plus in their relationship and you are likely to hear phrases like "mutual goals," "common purpose," "mission," or "shared vision." It is their fused visions that propel them to synergistic success.

"A task without a vision is drudgery"

*C*onjoint dreams do not imply sameness; they suggest reciprocity and mutuality. They are the symbiosis side of accord. They are communal. And they are shared — out loud. No, this does not mean you pull your customer aside and say, "You tell me your dreams and I'll tell you mine!" It *does* mean working hard to learn your customer's aims, goals, and aspirations. And it means letting customers know some of yours. It especially means exploring the front end (the "we" end) of welfare — how can we operate in a manner that contributes to our common well-being? Partner action without partnership vision can be unfocused, random effort.

At its core, purpose is an agreed-upon understanding of what is and is not important to creating a desired end. It is *the* tool for focus. If you have ever gone to a library in search of a specific journal article or technical book, and ended up sidetracked by a bound volume of twenty-year-old *Life* magazines, you know the price of wavering focus.

A partnership purpose gives individuals alignment and grounding. Alignment means laser-like, directed energy rather than scattered effort. It makes for work performed deliberately, efficiently, and precisely. Purpose is also a boon to grounding — as in "having one's feet on the ground" and "knowing what one is about."

Purpose is not only a synonym for vision and mission, it is often substituted for the word "focus." The oft-quoted "working on purpose" is an attempt to cleverly capture the double meaning of "focus": aligned or precise (i.e., on *purpose*) and grounded or relevant (*on* purpose). In a sentence, purpose lends meaning to a partnership. A purpose is about a dream — as in an aspiration or aim.

What does a clear customer-partnership purpose do for you and how is it crafted and communicated? An organization can elect any purpose. Ford Motor chose quality ("is job one"), the Marine Corps elitism ("a few good men") — at least it seems so from their advertisements. However, a partnership purpose is not about ad copy; it is what partners talk about and get excited about.

There are some intriguing litmus tests for partnership purposes. Ask the janitor who is busy on the business end of a broom what is most important to the organization. Janitors usually know! Or reflect on the last several meetings and try to recall the overriding themes, the subjects that captured air time. Or examine what type of error or mistake is likely to produce the quickest ire or most anxiety-related "wind-sucking." Or notice the subject of most reports that are circulated and dissected. What gets delighted comments? Disdainful curses? The answers to all these questions will tell you whether there is a purpose and what it might be.

A solid purpose need not be complex, academic, vague, or esoteric. Country Kitchen Restaurant's purpose is a good example:

> We make a very simple promise to all our guests:
> that our Country Kitchen is a warm, friendly place

where you'll always feel welcome, just like in your mom's kitchen. Come in any time of the day for meals cooked the way you like them, made from only the finest ingredients and always served with a smile. Good food, satisfying helpings, and fair prices. Thanks for coming into our Kitchen.

Such a clear statement of purpose leaves little doubt of what this organization is trying to be for its customers. After reading it, you would hardly expect a Country Kitchen restaurant to look, smell, or feel like a McDonald's or a five-star Chez Ronaldo.

A statement of purpose isn't necessarily a single, brilliant blanket statement covering all actions and applying to all people in the organization. However, the terms "simple," "concise," and "memorable" are all important. Too many organizations try to wrap a short blanket statement of purpose around multiple businesses with diverse products and services. They wind up publishing an embarrassing banality like "Service is our number-one mission." At worst, such a watered-down, all-encompassing effort fails to pass the "snicker test" with employees; at best, it fails to aid in directing effort or inspiring partnership.

Some organizations develop a purpose that gets wired into their ads. Eddie Bauer is a major mail-order catalog and chain of retail stores similar to the popular L. L. Bean Company. Eddie Bauer professes, "Our creed is to give you such outstanding quality, value, service, and guarantee that we may be worthy of your high esteem. We guarantee every item we sell will give you complete satisfaction or you may return it for a full refund."

Precision LensCrafters, a fast-growing, Cincinnati-based chain of optical supply stores, couples a promise on behalf of its customers with one made to employees. "PLC exists to develop enthusiastically satisfied customers *all* the time and to provide associates with a working environment which supports and encourages the development and achievement of their personal goals."

LensCrafters follows its service focus with a set of ten beliefs ranging from "Demand the highest possible quality" to "Accept mistakes" to "Have fun!"

But having a dream is not enough; the dream must be lived through actions. When *Inc.* magazine asked Bombay Company CEO Robert Nourse to describe his management style, he said, "Right from the beginning, I've had a vision of what this business is, and I tell people about it, and I believe in it, and I'm incredibly confident that it's right. And I've got a bunch of people here who share that conviction. That's an important driving force for a business."

Horst Schulze, president of the 1992 Malcolm Baldrige National Quality Award–winning Ritz Carlton Hotels, makes a big deal about partnering with new employees through new-employee orientation. "It all starts on their first day," he says. "There is no other moment in an employee's tenure with the hotel when he will be more attentive. If only *I* know the common goal, and I use everyone else to get there, then others are just tools. We must involve people and find consensus about our mission and the way to achieve it."

While Martin Luther King put "I have a dream" into words, every great service leader has the same perspective. A synergistic vision is the building block of partnerships, whether customer, corporate, or companion.

81

**❝ *When there is no vision,*
the people perish. ❞**
— Proverbs 29:18

Chapter 11

PROFILE IN PURPOSE: JOHN LONGSTREET

URPOSE-SEEKING LEADERS come in many forms. Some are swash-buckling and colorful. The late Bill McGowen, who founded MCI Tele-communications, was that way. In the early days of MCI, its suppliers would remark, "They did not always know what they were doing, but they were all clear on where they were going." CEOs Bill Young of Central Maine HealthCare, Hugh McColl of NationsBank, and Horst Schulze of Ritz Carlton Hotels are in the same spirited camp.

Some purpose-seeking leaders are quiet and reserved — Ban Hudson of U.S. Shoe and Jim Manzi of Lotus are examples. Some, like former

Chrysler CEO Lee Iacocca and General Electric CEO Jack Welch, communicate with laserlike directness. But whether loud, quiet, direct, or subtle, they all share one thing: they are clear on their vision and enfold vendors, employees, customers, and well-wishers in that "distant gate."

John Longstreet is one of my favorite examples. Few leaders can match his infectious enthusiasm and commitment. He is a quiet listener, a driven evangelist, and an assertive coach with a passion for purpose. John is the general manager of the Harvey Hotel in Plano, Texas. His property has one of the highest occupancy rates in the Dallas area and an extremely low employee turnover rate in an industry known for high turnover.

I first learned of John's special style when I was a frequent guest at the Harvey long before moving to Dallas. I got firsthand experience with his secret — creating a strong partnership with employees so they would create a similar partnership with guests. I was so impressed with the Harvey experience that I began to ask John to speak to my service management training classes held at the hotel. He never ceased to inspire, because participants could walk out of the meeting room and directly experience the results of John's leadership.

What follows are some of John's partnership practices, interspersed with his words. His approach makes clear to all the clear and focused connection between leader vision and customer memory.

"The essence of service, in my estimation, is making other people feel good. And I don't think it is a whole lot more complicated than that. Virtually all that I do is try to reinforce that simple but powerful principle. I believe the vast majority of people in the world are people who, if given a choice, would prefer trying to make other people feel good rather than making them feel bad. Most people are givers; a few are takers. We work hard to get more than our share of the former. And I work hard to give to them

so they stay inclined to give to our customers, our guests. Our guests return the gift through their return and their positive comments to others about our hotel."

Partnership at the Harvey begins with selection. I learned quickly that John places enormous emphasis on early identification of the talent unique to the culture of Harvey. John selects slowly. There is no "love at first sight" or "shoot from the hip" in his approach to hiring at the Harvey. Partners are careful in choosing colleagues.

"We are careful in who we choose. We want employees who are givers, those who seem to have a desire to partner with an organization dedicated to exceeding guest expectations. We accomplish this through team-talk interviews. The human resources manager initially screens the applicant. If the applicant looks like a keeper, he assembles the team. This includes the department manager where the individual will be working, another manager from another department, plus a would-be peer of that applicant. Hopefully, it will be someone who is excellent at his or her job. The team wants to get to know the person to determine if he or she is one of the 80 percent who are givers."

85

John's partnership effort continues from selection to orientation. He invited me to sit in on one of his new-employee orientations. I was particularly impressed with his insistence on "No, please call me John, we are on the same team." He warmly welcomed new employees, told them the history of the organization, and then excitedly launched into his unique view of purpose.

Later, John explained to me his role:

"My role as the service leader is to help new employees know that they have one goal — to make the guest feel good. My job is to help them understand that we truly

mean what we say. We work hard to give new employees powerful tools which begin to communicate that this organization is really different. The first tool we give them is 'throwing away the organizational chart.' We present the traditional organizational chart. Then we show them the 'Exceeding Guest Expectations' organizational chart — that being the dot of 'Exceeding Guest Expectations' in the middle, and then all of the employees and managers side by side trying to converge on that dot, trying to reach the common goal of 'exceeding guest expectations.'"

Harvey employees are not encumbered by job descriptions as we know them — that is, task-oriented job descriptions.

"Their job is simply to exceed guest expectations, and that remains the same for everyone in the hotel. When every position has the same job description, it becomes very clear that when a guest needs something, wherever you may be, you stop and take care of him. That is what causes the houseman to get down off the ladder when he is washing windows to open the door for a guest. His job description is not to wash windows; his job description is to exceed guest expectations.

"One of the key parts of the 'Exceed Guest Expectations' chart is that it has different applications for different people. The dishwasher exceeds the waiter's expectations in supporting the waiter's goal of exceeding guest expectations. So it is an exceeding-guest-expectations organizational chart — and philosophy.

*"Orientation is an opportunity to give employees the four keys to exceeding guest expectations. The first is to **be a risk taker** — to do things that may be against the rules but that will exceed guest expectations. I tell new employees, 'You can break a rule to exceed guest expectations; you can do anything you want to do to exceed guest*

expectations as long as it is not illegal or immoral, and as long as you have used your best judgment in making that decision.'

"The second key to exceeding guest expectations is to **be friendly.** The number-one comment we get from our guests is that our people are friendly. The third key is to **be sincere.** You've got to believe in the product (in our case, the service). If you don't believe in the product, change it so you can believe in it. And every person at this hotel has the ability to make changes, just as much so as the general manager. Like passengers on a train, any one of our employees can 'stop our train' should she feel it necessary.

"The fourth key is to **relax and have fun.** Employees who are having fun come across that way to the guests. People like to be around people like that. I like to tell all my employees, especially new employees, that I have two important goals as general manager. The first is to create an environment that is such a great place to work, people will be standing in line to try to get a job at the Harvey Hotel. The second goal is to create the kind of place where the general manager and the dishwasher are working side by side as partners on behalf of the guests. If I can do those two things, we will have no difficulty exceeding guest expectations."

87

Many managers talk like John, but few walk the talk like John. When he first became the general manager, he realized there was not an open, trusting environment, despite the fact that the previous manager had claimed he had an "open door" policy. John contacted the hotel engineer and informed him that he intended to have a "no door" policy. "Please remove my office door from the hinges!" he said. And John's office is in the very center of the executive office section, just off the lobby of the hotel. His flamboyant action communicated with a fresh new style that he was very serious about partnering with employees to exceed guest expectations. Partners don't need closed doors — or "open door" policies. They *are* open.

But I'll let John explain:

"The biggest obstacle to having employees treat customers like partners is the manager. It used to be that managers thought their role was to tell people what to do, and it was employees' role to do what they were told. That does not work anymore. The manager's job is to coordinate the work for a group of hopefully supercharged people out there breaking their backs to find ways to exceed guest expectations, and turning that effort into a profit. The leader's role is to eliminate obstacles, freeing employees to do well what they have been trained to do, and what they want to do.

"Managers have a tendency to want to treat employees like they are employees, not like they are partners in a common effort to exceed guest expectations. That is probably the hardest thing to retrain in an old manager. But it can be done — because in time he can see the effectiveness of a partnership approach rather than a bossing approach.

"Our employees are the reason why we are successful, and we must treat them like the most important people in our world. In my world, as the senior leader, the employees have to be more important than the guests, even. Because without the employee, we wouldn't have the guest."

John is an ardent fan of feedback. One exercise I used in classes on service quality was to ask participants to pay particularly close attention to all the tiny details the hotel did well or poorly that affected their experience. After being at the hotel for a day or so, I invited John to join my class and hear participants' feedback. Typically, he brought one of his other staff members. My classes were always impressed with how open and nondefensive

John was to their pickiest feedback. They also noticed his deep respect for his people.

"A manager's four commitments to his or her employees are to be hands-on and involved, to be supportive of good efforts even if they don't work, to be responsive to suggestions, and to be constantly rewarding people who exceed guest expectations.

"I believe that if you want employees to exceed guest expectations, you have to exceed employee expectations. The hands-on approach works like magic. Nothing makes employees more excited and inspired than when managers work in partnership with them, side by side. It can be as simple as pouring coffee for fifteen minutes at a busy time in the restaurant. Or opening a door for a guest. Or carrying a bag for a guest. I like that expression that our managers carry bags and our bellman makes executive decisions. It couldn't be a truer statement.

89

"One way I like to show that our employees come first goes like this: An employee walks into my office and asks, 'May I make an appointment to see you?' I say to him, 'Sit down, let's talk about it now.' It shows him that he is more important than anything in my day. I do not want to send him back out preoccupied with how he is going to discuss this with me."

One special treat I enjoyed with the Harvey Hotel was a chance to sit in on one of John's "What's Stupid" meetings. John holds monthly meetings with employees to get their input, suggestions, and critique on what needs to be done to help them exceed guest expectations. It was a powerful partnership forum. People were open and candid; John was curious and inquisitive. His favorite response to even the most negative comment was, "That's great, tell me more." The tenor of the meeting said a great deal about John's commitment to a true partnership with employees.

"I think another important aspect in creating a culture of partnership is communication. You've got to have open lines of communication. You've got to have an environment in which people feel they can say whatever they want without fear of recrimination. Where people can complain if they feel there is a problem. That's not done simply by having an open door. The way it is really done is by going out and asking them. Once you get the feedback, do something about it. Act on it. For goodness sake, the worst thing that can happen is for someone to provide feedback to a manager and then get in trouble for providing the feedback."

I have watched John pick up trash in the lobby. I have seen him give the Harvey Hotel Rose Award to an employee who went the extra mile for a guest. I have watched John serve coffee to guests and interview them about their stay. I have talked with countless employees over several years. They always speak of John as an endearing friend, an enduring partner. "He works so hard to make it easier for us to serve guests. I guess you might say we are his guests. He has such great confidence in us," said Marletta Smith, front-desk manager.

And what does John say?

"The decision-making process at the employee level is a crucial part of our culture. I believe empowerment cannot be conditional; it must be unconditional, or you are not really empowered. You can't say to a front-desk clerk, 'You can do whatever it takes to make this guest happy, up to twenty-five dollars.' If you are really going to empower an employee, she has to be able to do whatever it takes to make the guest happy. This is a scary thought for most managers, that it can actually work. It is also a scary thought for most employees. Consequently, given that authority, they are more likely to use good judgment and come up with a less expensive fix for the problem than if given some arbitrary number they have to work

within. They will always go up to the maximum on that arbitrary number."

One thing I learned from John is the importance of having a partnership ethic. It is an overriding allegiance to doing the right thing. And John demonstrates great faith that his employees — those givers who get selected for the Harvey partnership — intuitively know the meaning of the "right thing." He puts his trust in that fact.

"I think 'right' is an important aspect — that we do what we do based not on what is expeditious, or on what is cost effective, or on what we can get away with, but on what is the right thing to do. Employees are smart enough to sense when an organization really believes in that philosophy, when leaders actually honor that belief. And that is another thing that inspires them to do the right thing.

"We have one singular focus we want all our employees to demonstrate all the time. That happens by always talking about it, always role modeling it, always trumpeting our successes, always overreacting to make it right when we screw up, by my getting involved with every guest complaint. These are the kinds of things that show that single-minded focus on exceeding guest expectations and helping people feel good.

"Employees act like partners when leaders treat them like partners and give them an opportunity to help guests feel that same partnership feeling. We have one purpose and focus at the Harvey — and we are successful if that purpose permeates everything we say and do, every hour, every guest, in every way."

66 *The secret of success is constancy of purpose.* 99

— Benjamin Disraeli

Chapter 12

PROFILE IN PURPOSE: SHARON DECKER

SHARON ALLRED DECKER is the vice president of customer service for Duke Power Company, headquartered in Charlotte. Duke Power is considered one of the most progressive companies in its industry, and at Duke Power, Sharon is considered a groundbreaker.

Her passionate commitment to partnership with employees and with customers has put her out on the occasional limb. But it has paid off: General Electric's Answer Center, a customer-service exemplar to many folks, used Duke Power's Customer Service Center as *its* benchmark.

Sharon is a dynamo. She is one of those rare native-born Southerners who can speak at 78 rpm instead of 33. She also has an uncanny ability to talk on the phone, work on her computer, and deal with a steady stream of questions from "teammates" (employees) and "coaches" (supervisors) — simultaneously. Yet when she sits down to talk with you, she gives you her undivided attention.

I caught up with her during one of her quick stops in her unpretentious office in the middle of the Customer Service Center. She agreed to tell me what customer partnership means to her and to the Duke Power Customer Service Center. "Let me tell you a story," she began.

"We had an eighty-eight-year-old woman telephone our center complaining that her power was out. She was a big Washington Redskins football fan and the game was just about to begin. 'I'm not going to have too many more of these to watch,' she told our customer-service representative, 'and I want my power on now!'

"Our rep listened carefully and realized the issue was less about electricity and more about missing the game. The rep told the woman, 'I'll do everything I can to get your power on quickly. In the meantime, I'll call you every five or six minutes and update you on the score.' By the fourth quarter, the power was back on. The Redskins lost that day, but Duke Power and the customer won — a partnership was created.

"Customer partnership means building relationships with customers based on meeting needs that we each have, and creating opportunities for success, both for our customers and for Duke Power. Bottom line, it means caring deeply for the customer."

She paused and spoke with deep conviction. "In the final analysis, it's about . . . love." How does she communicate that conviction to employees? She is a leader who "walks her talk."

"When a teammate approaches me with a question or need, she watches first how I listen, and then how quickly and consistently I respond. I try to model the kind of behavior I want her to demonstrate with our customers.

"And there is more. 'Walking the talk' can mean simply being around. It can be as ordinary as eating lunch with whoever happens to be in the cafeteria and talking about their needs so I can identify opportunities to better serve them. You see, my teammates are my customers. I am here to serve them. I often joke that Sharon Decker could disappear and it might be several months before the effect would be noticed. But let one customer-service specialist miss a day of work and that's over a hundred customers that day who have to wait in queue on the telephone. That matters. My role is to support them so they can do their very best in serving our customers.

"I try to 'catch folks doing things right,' as some-one said, and to celebrate the good things instead of focusing on the negative."

Sharon aims at creating a culture in the Customer Service Center in which people know they have the support they need to take risks — a practice she encourages.

"When a mistake is made, we use it as a valuable learning opportunity. That makes any partnership work better. We want the partnership we have with each other as teammates to support them in creating partnerships with our customers."

One way she maintains internal partnerships with her team is by holding VIP luncheons.

"Once a month I have a luncheon with a select group of my internal customers — a random-draw kind of thing. The whole purpose is to listen to them — to hear what

things are on their mind, and find out what I as their team leader can do that would better support them in serving the customer. This is another way to 'walk the talk,' a way to exhibit the empathy and understanding that folks are asked to give our customers every day."

Of course, Sharon's passion for partnership also extends to external customers. She has come up with some powerful and innovative ways to ensure that the Customer Service Center is partnering with customers.

"We have customers participate in round-table and focus-group discussions. We also encourage them to come visit our Customer Service Center. We want customers to understand what we are trying to do. As they visit, we ask them to share their ideas and suggestions."

96   In an effort to keep tabs on their experiences and attitudes, the Customer Service Center solicits comments from customers within twenty-four hours of their contact with Duke Power.

"By actually talking with customers we have recently touched, we get powerful information on opportunities for improvement. Another way we stay updated on our customers' needs is by going out and listening to them, particularly our large industrial customers. This is a key to customer partnership. We know that if we can help our customers succeed in their businesses, we are going to succeed in ours. So it is in both our interests to really develop partnerships to help each other. We are listening more to our customers through these on-site visits and we are logging 'type of call' information as customers call us so we can identify recurring trends or problems."

Duke Power's Customer Service Center has also introduced another customer partnership idea it calls the

"Board of Customers." It asks customers within its three regions who represent a variety of demographic variables to attend a quarterly "board meeting" and spend a couple of hours giving the company feedback about new technology and about existing service.

"For instance, when we introduced a new voice-response unit, we ask our Boards of Customers, 'What do you think about it? How would you change the scripting? How can we better use this technology to meet your needs?' As we look at new products and services, we'll ask the Boards of Customers their opinions and ideas. That way, when we go to the market with a new service, we are more assured it will meet their needs."

How does Duke Power persuade customers to participate? It pays them thirty-five dollars if they travel less than twenty miles to the meetings and fifty dollars if they travel more than twenty miles, but customers agree to attend the meetings because they are approached as partners. "We say, 'We'd really love your feedback,'" explained Sharon. "We've built good relationships with our customers, and when we ask for their help, we get it."

Despite these innovative ways to reach out to customers, Sharon considers the best partnering with customers the kind that occurs on the spot, with quick-thinking customer representatives. And the center's "Bright Ideas" program gives reps a quick way to pass on great partnership ideas to co-workers. Sharon offered another story to illustrate her point:

"Some time ago during a power outage, one of our customers was quite concerned that if the power came back on in the middle of the night, he would have no way to know when to get up in order to get to work on time. The rep listened carefully to his concern and offered to give the customer a wake-up call the next morning. The customer

97

was elated, the rep shared the idea with others, and now a wake-up call is a standard service we offer customers during an evening power outage."

Despite the center's successes, Sharon is a firm believer in continuing to challenge her team to become ever more service sensitive.

"Our biggest challenge has been getting past our history as a protected monopoly. Our customers have told us in the past that we provided good service, but that perception of service was based on an expectation that utilities are pretty lousy service providers. Maybe we were the 'best of the worst.' The biggest challenge has been creating a climate where folks accept that 'good' just isn't good enough, that we should take pride in our heritage, but as more customers have choices, we have to get better and better at meeting and exceeding needs."

98

She has come up with several ways to maintain the excitement and intensity of the folks who serve customers. One is celebrating.

"We have Quality Days where we celebrate our progress as well as our success. I think there is a tendency in a lot of organizations not to celebrate because they are not there yet — not yet perfect. But to keep folks motivated, I believe you have to identify the progress and celebrate the fact that you've continued to move in a positive direction.

"We sometimes celebrate in crazy ways. Whether it's the leadership team dressing up for a fun skit or parading through the Customer Service Center with a kazoo band — whatever it takes to celebrate the team, have some fun, and create excitement for the vision of excellence in customer service."

Another way the center keeps employees excited is to involve them in decisions.

"We have lots of action teams — we call them 'A-Teams' — to get folks excited through an opportunity to participate in decision making. A-Teams were inspired by the television program. You remember, they were very focused, quick, effective, the good guys always won, and nobody ever got killed on that program. Those are the characteristics we want for our action teams."

Sharon is the youngest vice president at Duke Power and one of only a handful of female executives at her level in the industry. But she's not interested in talking about her successes. She prefers to focus the spotlight on her teammates. "They are the reason for our successes, not me," she insisted. So when I asked her what kind of customer-service legacy she would hope to leave, she struggled for a moment to come up with an answer that focused on Sharon Decker rather than on others.

"I would like to be remembered as a very caring leader who had a very clear vision of how exciting and beneficial real care and compassion for customers can be to our company and to the people who provide that service. I would like to be known as a leader who demonstrates that when a leader cares for employees, they will care for our customers.

"If my employees know that I love and appreciate them, that I am fair, that I am willing to coach for their continued growth, that I am flexible with them (we have twenty-two different work schedules), that I am willing to address problems when necessary, that I show compassion and understanding — then that is exactly what they are going to show Duke Power's customers."

Sharon dreams of a culture in which everyone sees service as an opportunity, not as an obligation.

"I contend that if people don't believe they can really be the very best, and don't believe in their heart that service

is important, then they can't provide a sense of partner-ship with customers. It has to do with who we are, not what we say."

She paused for a moment, then offered one last story to illustrate this dream:

"One of our reps called a delinquent customer who had not paid her bill in a couple of months. The customer pleaded for special assistance. The rep carefully listened and learned the customer was truly in a desperate situa-tion. The rep contacted several community assistance agencies, which resulted in the customer's getting finan-cial aid.

"Now, here is the real service part of the story. The rep and her teammates 'adopted' the family for Christmas and provided them toys and a Christmas dinner.

"My dream is to have a culture in which every rep, every coach, demonstrates that attitude every day to every customer, and shows that same attitude to his or her teammates. If our customers experience that kind of partnering, we will truly be the company of choice. When our customers have a choice in their utility, they will stay with us because we care.

"If there is one legacy I would hope to leave the Duke Power Customer Service Center, it is that I contrib-uted to that kind of culture by the way I showed care to my teammates."

100

❝The smallest good deed is better than the grandest good intention.❞

— Joseph Duquet

TRUTH

truth *n.* 1. Reality; actuality.
2. Sincerity; integrity; honesty.

I Am Truth

I am truth, I'm here to serve
    relationships, for they deserve
the special gifts that I convey;
    I change them to the partner way.

In courtrooms all across the land,
    they call me "whole" on witness stands.
It means complete, no fact concealed,
    for wholeness frees and wholeness heals.

In carpentry I represent
    a term for "level," nothing bent.
Truth provides all partnerships
    the lessons learned from candid lips.

For friendships I'm the color blue,
    I stand for steadfast, constant, true.
Partnerships require the same,
    a faith that says, "We will remain."

They reference me in history
    with George who axed the cherry tree.
All customers like honesty,
    and folks with bold humility.

If partnership's your foremost aim,
    remember truth can help you gain.
Your customers will loyal be,
    and thank you for including me.

Chapter 13

THE POWER OF MASK REMOVAL

WELCOME TO THE HARRY Thompson School of Selling! Harry is the president of Thompson-Mitchell, a large film distributor headquartered in Atlanta. An extraordinary service provider for many years, Harry is currently one of the country's leading distributors of training films.

Many years ago I had a real job: training director for a large North Carolina–based bank. Harry would occasionally call on me to sell me training films for workshops and seminars. Although the bank was very large, we were a very small customer, buying at best a film a year. But I was a big fan and a student of Harry's style of selling and serving.

I also became a fan and champion of Thompson-Mitchell, singing their praises to fellow trainers in other companies, many of whom bought lots of films. It was all due to loyalty to Harry.

The secret to Harry's impact on customers was revealed to me one day when the training director of a major utility and I were discussing Harry. We had both seen Harry at a training conference where he was an exhibitor. "He makes me feel so clean," the training director said. I thought to myself, "What an intriguing and graphic description!" However, it exactly captured my experience with Harry and was the primary cause of my allegiance to him.

Harry was real! No, I don't mean open or candid or honest, though he was all of those things. Harry was authentic — genuine and pure. His manner and style gave all who encountered him what felt like a clear window to his soul. There was never any effort to play a role or act like a salesperson or show off. Harry had mastered the art of mask removal. What you saw was what he was. His customers quickly became partners, and they removed their masks as well.

Partners check their egos at the door

*P*artnerships are obviously based on trust. But what is the origin of trust? We do not generally jump head first into a relationship. We go through a gradual toe-wetting stage to gain experience. Promises kept, expectations met, and dreams coming true all allow us to wade deeper into the relationship. One day we find ourselves in deep water together, yet feeling comfortable and safe.

But in the beginning, the toe wetting requires some risk. The ego-checking dimension serves partners as a lighthouse — a symbol indicating safe harbor. When I drop

my protection, I telegraph humility. It is confident realness. It is the opposite of arrogance and elitism.

Compare the negative reaction Exxon received over
the *Valdez* tragedy with the positive reaction Johnson &
Johnson received over the Tylenol tragedy. The difference
lies less with culpability and more with the authenticity
of communication. As Exxon opted for delayed vagueness
(some labeled it arrogance), Johnson & Johnson chose
humility and assertive realness. Look at before-and-after
market shares and see who won with the consumer!

On an American Airlines flight from Dallas to New
York, I watched an irate passenger board the plane and
curtly announce that American had done him in again. "I
have *had* it with this airline; three times and you're *out!*"
For three weeks in a row, he had failed to get the aisle
seat his long legs desperately needed. The flight attendants
promised to try to get him an aisle seat. Just before the plane
was ready to depart, the flight attendants realized there
was an aisle seat — *in first class!* He was escorted from coach
and served a drink. Now here is the key part: when the
captain announced a brief delay in departure, one flight
attendant purposefully approached him, stooped to his
eye level, and asked him how he was doing. She sincerely
and intently listened to his story. He obviously felt moved
by her interest and finished his "life is a bitch" story by
saying, "but I'm gonna stay with American and tell my management to make you our primary carrier." It was clearly
not the upgrade or free drink that sealed the turnaround —
it was the authentic caring delivered with simple sincerity.

Mask removal is caring enough to let go

A Hawaiian woman who spoke limited English
was en route to Roanoke, Virginia, to visit
her daughter. After six thousand miles, eighteen hours,

and four stops, she arrived in Charlotte, only to learn that the Roanoke Airport was closed due to snow and ice. On the last leg of her journey and now only one hour from her destination, she was informed that she would have to stay the night in Charlotte. A USAir gate agent made all arrangements, called her daughter for her, then sat with her for a while, asking the woman questions about Hawaii and her daughter. As tears welled up in the woman's eyes, the gate attendant spontaneously embraced her and said, "You've come so far, I know you really want to see her." The woman smiled through her tears and said in broken English, "I'm glad you are my friend."

Think about the service partnerships you have enjoyed in the past. There was no doubt about the service provider's caring; your partner regularly demonstrated caring by a willingness to "surrender" with you — not to you. It is selfless, not compliant. It is doing what is needed, rather than what is rewarded. It is running relationships based on other-interest magic rather than balance-sheet logic. It is an act of bequest, not an act of allowance, loan, or favor. True partners worry less about who owes whom and focus more on "How can I help or support?"

One Friday evening I arrived home from a long, difficult week of consulting. The normal "tradversities" of living out of a suitcase five nights in four hotels in three cities had been combined with two delayed flights, terrible weather, and a persistent head cold. My wife met me at the front door with my favorite refreshment, and insisted that I skip the stack of a week's worth of mail I had vowed to dig through and move to our back yard for some late-night jacuzzi. Near midnight, I realized my feet were prunes and she had patiently listened to an hour of my story, and I had not asked her one single question.

"And how was your day?" I asked with embarrassment. "That's okay," she said with a knowing smile. "You needed to unload. Let's go to bed and I'll tell you tomorrow." Nancy was willing to surrender her need for reciprocal now-it's-my-turn for caring service.

Harry Thompson has a lot in common with Nancy. He sometimes came by and spent the entire visit listening to me bitch and/or brag, and never even brought up his "Let me tell you about our new. . . ." Harry might get a D-minus in your organization's Super Selling Skills training course, but he was patiently demonstrating that he cared more about the customer than the sale. Customer caring was more valuable than contract closing. Yet I know for a fact that Thompson-Mitchell is a leader in the film sales and rental industry.

Mask removal is personified honesty

I have learned from my colleague Larry Davis in Austin, Texas, that trust has a lot to do with intention. My trust of you and yours of me is in part tied to my perception of your intention. Honorable intentions tell me how far to drop my guard when dealing with others. If I am trustworthy, that means I act in a manner that is so obviously honest that I communicate that I am worthy of your trust. It has a lot to do with how one feels about oneself.

109

People who cheat, lie, and deceive in relationships are communicating that they have such an inferior view of themselves that they deem they are not worthy of another's trust. So they act distrustful — that is, full of doubt and suspicion. Self-doubt breeds distrust. Mask removal starts with the premise that I feel positive about myself, positive enough to risk (i.e., trust) that your motives are equally pure. If I am willing to trust, I will receive authenticity in return.

On one of Harry Thompson's "How's it going?" visits, he remembered I was particularly interested in any film that helped male managers understand and manage their biases about the upward mobility of women (this was in the early 1970s). "Chip, I brought you this new copy of *Fifty-One Percent*," he announced. "Use it in your next workshop and let me know what you think. I believe you'll want to buy a copy." There was no mention of invoice, purchase order, or contract. And you can bet I bought a copy! Honesty is not only the best policy, it is the best precursor to partnership with customers.

Masks disguise our honest selves from others, sometimes unnecessarily and unintentionally. The observer-customer, however, perceives that masks hide our intentions and our motives. And goodness knows, anyone who wears a mask must do so because he or she needs to hide something. Therefore, anything less than authenticity conjures in customers' minds a whole array of sinister images that militate against partnership.

I saw Harry last month at a training conference. His exhibit-hall booth was jam-packed with fans and wannabe customers. "What's so special about that booth?" I heard a novice attendee ask an old hand. "Oh, that?" replied the veteran. "Folks are just wild about Harry!"

66 Chase after the truth like all hell and you'll free yourself, even though you never touch its coat-tails. 99

— Clarence S. Darrow

Chapter 14

CUSTOMER CANDOR

ONE OF THE SUREST signs of a bad or declining relationship with a customer is the absence of complaints. Nobody is ever *that* satisfied, especially not over an extended period of time. The customer is either not being *candid* or not being *contacted.*" These words of Harvard professor and marketing guru Ted Levitt were tucked in his pithy September–October 1983 *Harvard Business Review* article, "After the Sale Is Over . . ."

His message worried me for days! Here I was striving to minimize customer (a.k.a. client, partner, guest, patient, employee) irritation and ire only to have Levitt tell me that "no complaints" was something to be avoided, and it was *my* fault for not getting any! I was confused. Weren't we supposed to be seeking all A's, zero defects, 100 percent, a perfect ten, five stars, a hole in one? How can "getting more customer complaints" be a virtue? Can you imagine marching into the division head's office with the "good news" that complaints were up 23 percent and therefore you needed a bigger budget, more staff, and a large salary increase?!

Then I had one of those significant emotional experiences with my wife of now twenty-nine years. We were attending a weekend retreat associated with our son's school — sort of a family enrichment workshop. One assignment was for each of us to write a list of the strengths and limitations of the other members of the immediate family.

My wife and I enjoy a very open, honest partnership. Yet the pace of managing dual, fast-paced professional careers with typical family challenges can work counter to the late-at-night, no-kid-gloves honesty we desire. When she read my limitations out loud ("You sometimes focus so totally on your work that we don't get the attention we need" or "You go into too much detail"), it had a rather sobering effect on me! The exercise provoked a level of candor we had not had in a while.

I began to appreciate why Levitt compared a quality customer relationship to a marriage. "The sale consummates the courtship, at which point the marriage begins. The quality of the marriage depends on how well the seller manages the relationship," wrote Levitt. "The absence of candor reflects the decline of trust and the deterioration of the relationship."

Partners don't demand perfection

My weekend encounter prompted me to examine other pearls of customer partnership. Customers, like spouses, do not expect us to be perfect;

they just expect us to demonstrate that we care enough to strive to improve. When we demonstrate caring, customers reciprocate by caring enough to offer their feedback and suggestions. My wife's cataloguing of my improvement opportunities was not an act of critical judgment, but rather an act of caring and love.

Customer-service research directed by John Goodman, president of the TARP Institute in Washington, D.C., has unearthed several findings consistent with Levitt's *Harvard Business Review* pronouncement. Only 4 percent of a business's less-than-satisfied-customer complaints reach a person who could fix things. The great majority say, "Fine," when restaurant cashiers ask, "How was everything?" Customers would rather privately register their disapproval, with their feet, than publicly deliver their disdain directly to the front line. Why aren't customers truthful with us? The TARP Institute found three major reasons: customers don't know *how* to register complaints; they believe it won't really do any good; or they fear that the service provider might retaliate.

So why do service organizations or internal service units avoid assertively soliciting complaints? Perhaps some lull themselves into thinking, "No news is good news," or "Let sleeping dogs lie." Some fear that if they seek and receive customer complaints and then take no corrective action, they might be thought worse than if they had left bad enough alone. The research, however, does not support such an assumption. Better to have asked and not acted than not to have asked at all. Some have not figured out how to ask effectively for complaints without sounding almost masochistic. Some have asked incorrectly, failed to get helpful information, and simply given up asking.

The "better to have loved and lost" orientation is one consistent with solid service wisdom. Those customers who have been directly asked for feedback are much more likely to give favorable reviews than those who have not. Customers who have had a service problem and had it spectacularly corrected are more loyal than those who have never had a problem. According to TARP, only 9 to 37 percent of irate customers (depending on the dollar value of their problems) who don't complain will return to a service provider if nothing happens after they have been aggrieved. However, if there is a legitimate outlet for their ire, that return business jumps to almost 50 percent — even without correction of the service problem.

Complainers spend more than noncomplainers

114

*T*he most powerful statistic is that complainers are worth twice as much as noncomplainers with service problems in terms of previous purchases. It is not the one-time buyer who fusses and flees. Complainers are more typically customers who have spent lots of money in the past. Add up all those facts and figures and you get a convincing argument to go out and plead with your customers to "tell us how it really is."

The truth-seeking component of effective partnership is that which values candor and openness. It is the dimension that honors authenticity and realness. The path to truth in relationships is paved with interpersonal risk taking and mutual critique. It involves the courage to ask for feedback as well as the compassion to give feedback. Truth may sometimes leave relationships temporarily uncomfortable and bruised, but truth always leaves partnerships hearty and healthy. It exterminates guilt and deceit. Truth nurtures cleanness in associations.

George Washington University Business Professor Jerry Harvey's famous Abilene Paradox story is an instructive tool for examining customer partnerships. Now, if you have never actually read Jerry's story, I encourage you to buy a copy of *The Abilene Paradox and Other Meditations on Management*. Here's a short version of his story:

Jerry and his wife Betty were visiting her parents in Coleman, Texas. After a long, quiet afternoon of dominoes on the back porch in front of the fan, Betty's father suggested the four of them go fifty miles across the hot August desert and have dinner at the bus station cafeteria in Abilene. One by one, Jerry, Betty, and Betty's mother agreed to the trip.

After a miserable evening, they returned to Coleman to sit silently in front of the back-porch fan. One by one, each admitted he or she really had not wanted to go to Abilene in the first place. Even Jerry's father-in-law acknowledged he had not really wanted to go to Abilene but simply suggested it out of his concern that Jerry and Betty might be bored during their visit.

Like the Abilene Paradox, false agreement is a much greater threat to partnerships than honest conflict. Healthy candor means caring more about uncomfortable genuineness than amiable "white lies."

How do you get customers to level with you? My wife's approach to truth seeking may offer guidance for soliciting customer candor. She skillfully enticed me to deliver a more honest cataloguing of her improvement opportunities. When I made my first "Well, you sort of . . . , it's not a big deal, but. . . ." attempts to offer candid critique, she thanked me! "That is *very* helpful," she said. "Tell me more about that." Plus she gave me her undivided attention during my stammerings. She never once got defensive, even as I got bolder in my critique. She reiterated what she heard to let me know my feedback was understood. She never once tried to "set me straight" by explaining her actions. And she even occasionally "primed the pump" by putting on the table frustrations she already knew I had. "I know it sometimes bothers you when I. . . . What else like that bugs you?"

Here is the endearing part: she actually changed some of her actions based on my critique! Not everything, mind you — but certainly enough to let me know that my critique made a difference. So the next time she asked, "How can I improve?" I was much more assertive and complete in my candor.

Stew Leonard's Dairy Store in Norwalk, Connecticut, was listed in the *Guinness Book of Records 1994* as having the largest dollar volume per square foot of any retail establishment in the world. "We do it by listening to our customers," Stew explains. "Customers tell us what they don't like — and they tell us because we react to it." This is not to say Stew does exactly what every single customer suggests. But he acts on many of their comments. Most of his customers are convinced that Stew values their input — convinced enough to give the store gross receipts of almost $2 million a week.

No customer relationship is likely to be perfect all the time. The healthy customer partnership, like the healthy marriage, is marked by candor and welcomed critique. Honesty fuels more honesty if defensiveness is absent. As the relationship improves, the service-provider-to-receiver relationship evolves into a true partnership. And as candor triggers improvement, those who serve feel responsive, those served feel heard, and the partnership feels healthy. "Now, customer, tell me what you really, truly, no-holds-barred, honestly, think of our service!"

66 *The language of truth is unadorned and always simple.* 99

— Marcellinus

Chapter 15

LISTENING IS A CONTACT SPORT

I RECENTLY HAD MY ANNUAL physical examination. You know how these work: midnight-to-blood-test fasting equals a long delay on morning coffee. However, Nurse Julie became Saint Julie when, after taking two vials of blood, she very quickly returned with a large, hot cup of coffee. "As I remember, you like your coffee black," she announced with confidence. I felt heard — and valued.

Listening well is a rarity in our society. That, in part, explains the popularity of psychologists. Unfortunately, that in part also explains the divorce rate. And the fact that the largest share of self-help books on the bookstore shelves are about communication.

Listening does not mean corresponding. Listening does not mean simply looking at someone while she speaks to you. Listening means being actively engaged in the process of seeking to understand another person. Listening is not just about what you do, it is about what your partner experiences. It is, therefore, a contact sport. Listening without contact, without dramatic connection, is like looking without seeing. And given the uniqueness of being *really* heard, the customer will remember long those who listen well.

Customer partnerships require dramatic listening, the type that a customer experiences as "Wow, she *really* heard what I said." It is front-line employees who tune in rather than turn off. Remember the American Airlines flight attendant and the USAir gate attendant you met in chapter 13? Great listening is responsive and active.

Dramatic listening combines receptive with responsive

*D*ramatic listening marries input with interest. It includes thanking customers for their returned surveys, then letting them know what changed as a result of their input.

John Longstreet, the Harvey Hotel general manager you met in chapter 11, employs what he calls the "lobby lizard" program — a member of his management team (including John) works the lobby between 7:00 and 9:00 a.m. each day serving coffee and interviewing departing guests about ways the hotel could improve. The management team member also drives the courtesy van to the airport, with the same goal.

Erie "Chip" Chapman, CEO of U.S. Health Corporation, uses a similar practice, spending one day a week on the front lines, often wearing a volunteer's coat to reduce the odds that people (patients *and* employees) will edit what they're saying because they know who's listening.

Dramatic listening demonstrates lavish under-standing, which telegraphs to the customer, "I was paying attention when you least expected it." Dramatic listening in action is a personalized response that leaves the receiver a little awed by the incident. Sending the customer a birth-day card might be routine understanding; lavish is send-ing the customer a newspaper clipping on USC's new Art School building because you remembered the customer happened to mention that her son was considering the college and might want to major in art.

Doubletree Inns asks a first-time guest, "Would you like a complimentary plate of chocolate-chip cookies and a glass of milk before bedtime?" Doubletree's com-puters remember your preference, and each time you check into another Doubletree, the system makes sure milk and cookies are delivered to you.

Listening is axiomatic to customer partnership. Stop and think about this: What makes a partnership work? Whether you're talking about marriage, a business relationship, or a customer relationship, a key part is extraordinary communication. Partners expect you to work hard at listening and to act as though their input matters. Partners expect you to respond in a manner that lets them know you were listening.

119

Good partners don't bet the farm on survey results

*M*arket research is important, but it can seduce service providers into categorizing custom-ers and missing their individual uniqueness. "A market never purchased a single item in one of my stores," said Stanley Marcus, cofounder of Neiman-Marcus, "but a lot of customers came in and made me a rich man!" Market research also tends to present findings in a colorless way that misses the spirit of service. We need to really listen to capture the "blood and guts" of heart and soul.

At budget season, many ministers use the stewardship theme for their pledge-Sunday sermons. My minister on that particular Sunday made a strong point that the easiest route to stewardship is check writing. "This completely misses the point of our stewardship responsibility to each other and our partnership role with the community," said Dr. Leighton Ferrell of Highland Park United Methodist Church. He continued: "Stewardship is about personal actions and sacrificial energy. It is about putting energy into relationships, not about putting money into the offering plate."

Dramatic listening is cut from the same cloth. It cannot be accomplished through sterile surveys or clever comment cards. It is a living, personal, "skin in the game" encounter. Partners inquire up close, they don't survey at a distance.

Can you imagine the impact of ascertaining relationship needs and expectations in your most important relationship via techniques used by many service providers? "Honey, I need your candid feedback about how to improve our relationship. In the morning when you come down for breakfast, you will find, beside your cereal bowl, a survey and a number-two pencil. I have provided a postage-paid return envelope." If your situation is like mine, you would probably be eating the survey for breakfast! Surveys are not the partnership way. Partners do not listen at arm's length.

"But," you may respond, "we have thousands of customers. We have face-to-face encounters with only a very few." If your success depended on personal encounters with customers, what would you do differently? You might find ways to entice or encourage customers to initiate contact with you. You might equip front-line employees differently. You might find clever ways to bring customer and service provider closer together. You might craft correspondence to have more of a partnership tone, generated by people closer to the customer.

At one point in her career, my wife was a high-school principal. Periodically she ordered plaques, trophies, and awards from the Award Company of America in Tuscaloosa, Alabama. One dreary February she decided to order valentine-ribbon bookmarks for each member of her faculty. Valentine's Day marks the midpoint between the winter holiday break and spring break; teachers often need a pick-me-up. When the ribbons arrived, they were accompanied by a letter addressed to my wife:

Dear Dr. Bell:

Thank you for ordering gold-stamped ribbons from Award Company of America. I am the machine operator who actually made your ribbons. I am very proud of my work. My company and I guarantee the ribbons to be to your complete satisfaction.

We want to give you personal service. If you are dissatisfied for any reason, please contact our Customer Service department. They will contact me and I will personally correct any problem.

Thank you again for your order. We all look forward to receiving your next order.

Sincerely,

Susan Marcum
Ribbon Machine Operator

Instead of a corporate communication, she felt as though she had received a note from an Alabama neighbor. Corporate "we's" rarely connote empathetic ears; listening is a personal encounter. Regardless of the medium of communication, partnership listening is a "Letter from Susan" contact.

Great partnerships are built on honesty and mutuality. Both of these qualities are dependent on dramatic listening. Listening yields the candid, honest feedback that enables the service provider to correct, improve, and enhance. Listening provides the up-to-date awareness of partner needs and expectations that enables the service provider to align and attune.

Now, think about the primary way you "listen" in your organization. It is important that customer information has depth enough for sound decisions and breadth enough for fair decisions. What percentage of your listening is passive, indirect, and rational? What percentage is the opposite — active, direct, and emotional? Partnership listening is far more about contact and connection than calculations and charts.

❝ *Well timed silence hath more eloquence than speech.* ❞

— M. T. Tupper

BALANCE

balance *n.* 1. A state of equilibrium.
2. A harmonious or satisfying
arrangement or proportion of
elements.

Negotiable Bonds

There once was a traveling show
that knew only friend, never foe.
When this show came to town
all the folks gathered round
to transform to joy all their woe.

The clowns acted silly and fun.
A man was shot out of a gun.
The popcorn was hot,
the snow cones were not.
A magician made rabbits from none.

The circus had one special thing
that people said made them like kings.
Done partly as act,
but mostly as fact,
it made even grouchy folks sing.

The man who invented this act,
a banker was he and he lacked
a heart with his head,
a smile with his dread;
he trusted no person, just facts.

This banker had granted a loan
to one he forever had known.
The terms were as bait:
one single day late
and the banker took all the man owned.

The borrower pled for a break;
the banker said, "Jump in the lake,
this bond you did sign
meant there was a bind.
The facts are the facts, now I take."

The man, now a beggar, made bed
in the library basement, and read
   all the medical books,
    his passions were hooks
to know what was in doctors' heads.

The beggar soon read every page,
knew symptoms, the cures and the gauge.
   He wanted a chance
    his life to enhance,
but no one would help out this sage.

One dark day the banker's young lad
fell ill from a fruit he had had.
   The doctor was gone,
    the banker alone.
He ran through the streets as if mad.

The sound of his calling for aid
was chance that the beggar had prayed.
   The people would see
    a doctor was he;
he went where the boy had been laid.

The banker was awed by this sight:
the beggar who had every right
   to turn up his nose
    in anger from woes
this banker had caused by his might.

"Forgive me," the banker soon cried,
"The bond I laid on you I tied
   to thinking of me,
    not thinking of 'we';
negotiable bonds I'd not tried."

The beggar now doctors the sick.
The banker decided to pick
   a life in a show
   to help others know
negotiable makes all bonds tick.

Each show that the people attend,
the story is retold again.
   It gives them all hope,
   agreements with rope,
since partnerships last when they bend.

Chapter 16

THE PRONOUN IN POWER IS "WE"

*I*USED TO TELL AUDIENCES that service was about confident deference. Just plain "deference" sounded too servant-like. Just plain "confident service" sounded too presumptive. I thought the phrase made a lot of sense.

But that was before I met Dave Forrest.

When I first met Dave he was a franchise owner of a small printing shop in Charlotte — a quick-copy place, we called it. He learned early through his "What exactly do you do?" curiosity that I was involved in service quality. He quickly moved into action, picking my brain about some small aspect of his operation almost every time I came in. During my sometimes brief wait for copies he would show me his ideas for expansion and getting more customer oriented, then ask me sincerely, "What do you think?" I kept coming back to get his special "You got a friend" brand of service. His printing was never any cheaper or better than any other good printer, but he always served customers as though they were his best friends — everyone, not just me.

Forrest Graphics soon quadrupled in size and volume. When my colleagues and clients said, "I'll send it over to Dave and he'll print it for me," or "*My* printing company," I knew they too had been enfolded into Dave's brand of partnership. Dave deeply respected his customers (whom he always called clients). He also respectfully picked their heads for ideas and insights — and their hearts for inclusion and fidelity!

I realized I had graduated to Dave's VIP list one day when he gave me his business card with his home phone on the back and said, "Chip, with your travel schedule, I know you sometimes need stuff copied at odd times. My shop's not open on weekends, but feel free to call me at home if you have an emergency, and I'll be happy to open up for you." I did — and he did — more than once! Twice, I joined another "lucky partner" on a Sunday morning who also had an "Omigod" rush job.

You did not meet Dave on an emergency rendezvous to watch and wait, you met to hold and help. He expected you to labor *with* him in these "beyond the call of duty" moments. And the more you rummaged through Dave's stock room or searched the trunk of his car for a needed printing plate, the more you found yourself emotionally involved in Forrest Graphics as an equal partner.

I started sending Dave articles on small business operations. He called me at home a couple of times to ask me about an idea. My name made his Christmas list; I added him to mine. He held a customer-appreciation barbecue in his back yard and tons of people came out of the woodwork. Conversations with colleagues often turned to "Dave said . . ." or "Isn't Forrest Graphics something?" or "How can we help Dave?" We were all hooked — and, I might add, so was Dave. The partnership felt monogamous; none of Dave's clients would let anyone else do their printing.

Dave's brand of service quality came through something I call "e-quality." He was always respectful and confident, never deferential. He knew his survival depended on customers, but his success depended on partners. And partnerships were birthed through a recognition that, while service provider and customer were different, they could effectively operate in a context of parity. E-quality isn't something you read about in textbooks, but it's central to effective partnership.

Equality begins with respect

131

Customer partnerships don't begin as such. Like a marriage, the relationship rarely flips from "How do you do?" to "I do!" in one fell swoop. It starts with encounter, moves to experience, then to enjoyment, and somewhere along the way, to partnership. One key aspect of this journey is the demonstration of respect.

Respect is made of admiration, esteem, and honor. When we respect someone, we admire who he is and/or what he does. There is either an "I wish I could . . . like she can" kind of awe or an "I know how hard it is to . . ." connection. Dave admired my ideas about service quality; I admired his ability to make customers feel special. He actively demonstrated his admiration and I worked hard to do likewise.

Respect is also made of esteem and honor. To esteem or honor a relationship is to ascribe credit or adoration to it. It involves seeking ways to bring accolades and praise to the relationship. Dave would often speak admiringly of me to other customers when I was there. He was openly candid and genuinely grateful about my value to him and his business. I went out of my way to recommend Dave to others. And I would always give him tribute when his Sunday morning service got me out of a tight-deadline printing jam.

Equality requires participation

My neighbor Max has a large family scattered across Texas. Recently, his uncle had a serious illness — the kind that has family members sitting around the bedside expecting to hear the last gasp. Max expressed less than pleasure about going to visit. This surprised me, since I knew he was close to his family. "Oh, I want to see everyone and be with Uncle Neal," he said. "But Uncle Neal's family is so much in control and won't let you help or do anything for them — I feel more like a guest than a cousin."

It was a powerful reminder that equality requires invited and invested energy. You cannot witness your way into partnership; you've got to wet your feet. The "People will care if they share" adage is part of what gives a relationship depth and meaning. Partnership is not a spectator sport. Service providers who treat the customer like "Max, the guest" instead of "Max, the cousin" will never get the depth of commitment that partnership implies.

Dave always gave you an assignment when he was in his "Go the extra mile" stance. I got so accustomed to being "a member of the family" that I would find myself during normal business hours walking behind the counter to help collate a last-minute project for someone else while I waited for my order. "You don't have to do that," a Forrest Graphics employee would always say. But usually Dave would bellow from the back, "Aw, let him help, we need all of it we can get. Besides, Chip is family." Employees soon were treating me with a sense of kinship and admiration.

Partnership does not mean giving away your heart and soul to make the customer feel pleased. Partners ask for contribution when the scale gets too asymmetrical. While everyday equilibrium is not essential, partners do require relative balance. Powerful partnerships are made up of partners who assert with compassion rather than acquiesce in compliance.

Equality requires breathing room

You might suspect that in time Dave's employees lowered their excellence edge for me — "Oh, don't worry about that being top drawer, that's for ol' Chip and he won't care." But they *never* took me for granted. They never forgot that I had the freedom to bid them farewell at any juncture without notice.

133

Equality requires breathing room. Cut from the "respect" cloth, it is a relationship that gives homage to separateness while enjoying the benefits of mutuality. Smother customers and they will fly away. Take them for granted and they will steal away in the night without warning.

For four years I was working three to four days every month in Miami on a long-term consulting project. I chose an elegant, convenient hotel within walking distance of the client's headquarters office. I got to know everyone in the hotel and they me. It became my "home away from home." They would do favors for me; I sang their praises and brought them major meetings. After a year, however, the "shiny" wore off and I began to be treated too familiarly. Employees told me their hard-luck stories as though I were a fellow employee; one even gave me his résumé to help him find another job and leave the hotel. They once gave me a poor room when a key group of executives came in. Their explanation: "We knew *you* would understand

and not mind!" They didn't bother to ask me ahead of time! The punch line? I plotted my escape and switched hotels for the final thirty-six months of my Miami work.

Partnerships can never be consistently or perpetually equal. There is always a rise and fall; power shifts back and forth as the parties in the partnership seek to equalize their relationship with each other. Sometimes I felt Dave was assuming too much of me; sometimes, I am sure, he felt the same of me (especially on Sunday mornings!). But we valued the relationship enough to weather the few out-of-balance moments. And with some history, we soon developed the confidence that fostered tenacity and commitment.

An important part of partnership effectiveness is to pursue a goal of equality, using respect, participation, and breathing room as important tools in the exchange. The Dave Forrest approach helps ensure that the partnership will pay rich dividends for a long time.

134

I talked with Dave a few weeks ago when I called him to print some envelopes and ship them to me in Dallas. He had the same "Thank goodness you are my customer!" sound in his voice he had in 1980.

"When are you going to open a franchise in Dallas?" I teased him.

"When are you going to move back to Charlotte and help me make this shop better?" he responded in the same tone.

It was like a postcard from the old neighborhood — the powerful "we" spirit of mutuality without a scorecard.

66 *Without courage, all other virtues lose their meaning.* 99

— Winston Churchill

Chapter 17

FLOATING RECIPROCITY

ERITAGE CLEANERS is a sole-proprietorship, single-shop, mostly kinfolk-employees laundry that stands on the boundary between antique residential and modern industrial neighborhoods in Southeast Charlotte. Since I lived in one and worked in the other, Heritage was on my daily route. For a small extra price, I could even drop dress shirts off on my way to the office early morning and pick them up on my way home late afternoon. Paul Langford was the owner/greeter/server/order-giver at both ends of the day.

Paul was a master at surprising customers with more than they expected. One hot Sunday afternoon as I was packing for a hectic, five-day New York–D.C.–Los Angeles trip, I discovered I had failed to stop by Heritage on Friday afternoon and was short the suits I needed. I called Paul at home; he met me at his shop within minutes. Even though he closed at six, he would always wait fifteen or twenty minutes for me if I called as I left the office at 5:59 p.m. He once delivered my clothes to my home unrequested when he realized I had not come by at the end of the week, the upcoming Monday was a holiday, and he was holding clothes he thought I might need on Tuesday.

Then Heritage Cleaners had a fire. Though I don't recall the details, it turned out that a disgruntled ex-employee had set fire to the small, cinder-block building. Paul quickly negotiated an alliance with another laundry and set up his temporary shop in a house trailer he parked on the original parking lot. It was to be Heritage while the gutted building was rebuilt.

I felt for Paul. And I remained a customer, like others who made the same stop on Providence Road. After all, while he cracked my shirt buttons from time to time, and the press job was not always perfect, and he was a bit pricey, Paul always ran a fast extra mile for his customers.

Then one Saturday morning my "Stand by Paul" stance turned into devoted partnership. Heritage was open until noon on Saturdays and I stopped by the trailer for my clothes. Paul was there with his employee-son, Jamie. "Chip, have you got a few minutes?" he nonchalantly asked. I could read on Jamie's face that there was more hope that I would say "Sure!" than Paul wanted me to hear in his voice. "Sure!" I said.

An hour later, I left the trailer. Paul had fervently described the special challenge of trying to jump-start his formerly successful laundry business. It seemed the fire had burned enthusiasm and resolve along with equipment and roofing. I gladly shared some management lessons learned, insights acquired, and perspectives gained. Paul and Jamie listened intently to my ideas and took copious notes. When I had finished, their expressions of relief made me wonder if they had put far more reliance on my "top of mind" ideas than was warranted.

A few days later I stopped by the Heritage Cleaners trailer. It had a noticeably different feel to it; they greeted me more like a patron than a consumer. With pride they demonstrated how they had extended my ideas. They had taken my partially baked thoughts and raised them to a level of relevance for their customized challenge. My concepts had been squared and then cut a new way. I felt proud — like a new partner.

Thanks to a cooperative insurer, it was not long before Heritage reopened in its refurbished building. The place had retained much of the charm of its past, but with a clear eye toward modernization and growth. My first time in the place, Paul called me behind the counter and gave me the fifty-nine-cent tour. As I returned to the waiting area, a customer approached the counter and asked for her laundry. "You take this one," he told me. He excitedly walked me through the process as if I were a new employee, then said, "You are welcome on this side of the counter any time you like, Dr. Bell. You are our silent partner."

Partners care about fairness, not a fifty-fifty split

*P*artnerships are about floating reciprocity. The balance they enjoy is never perfect but always percolating. Just when you feel guilty for taking too much, an opportunity arises to even the score. Partners do not worry long about overdrawing; their relationship gives them overdraft protection. They know the roomy connection will help them make good on any out-of-balance situations that go on too long. Effective partnerships seek ways to help each partner contribute. Such relationships are grounded in optimism that says, "It will all balance out in the end," even if the concept of "end" is vague and imprecise.

Partners don't put much energy into contracts. They do value clear agreements and mutual understanding. And they also have a lot of faith. My partners and I have written many articles and books together. We have also developed a number of products — training programs, surveys, films, and the like. An obvious issue would be how to split royalties and recognition. Since we all have healthy egos, you might imagine there would be some concern over whose name goes first on a book or how to fairly split royalties. Many business partners would decide that issue up front; we always decide it after the fact! We trust that after the dust settles on each effort we can fairly decide based on contribution. Since 1986, there has never been a credit problem. And revenues are rarely split exactly even; books and articles I coauthor have my name first about as often as one of the other partners.

Sure, there are times when writing down agreements helps with fading memories. Certainly there are times when many people are involved and a meeting of the minds needs to occur beyond the authors of the deal. Real partners, however, do not worry much about the deal-making, contract-management side of their relationship.

Where did written contracts originate? They emerged from a betrayal of the fairness doctrine: someone cut the candy bar *and* took the first piece! Betrayal is the enemy of floating reciprocity.

Betrayal most often is a manifestation of greed and power. It can also be a clear and present demonstration of the abuse of trust. Whatever the origin, betrayal violates the sanctity of "A person's word is her bond." Solid partners honor their word-bond against all odds and ends.

Customers value service providers who avoid the "pound of flesh" mentality. When the "balance the books" bean counters of the organization search for all the pennies in customer transactions, they risk losing the dollars of a loyal customer who desires a relationship with a bit more give in it.

Equality has nothing to do with rules

Several years ago my wife and I bought an industrial-strength sofa/hideabed and had it delivered to our rustic Lake Wylie retreat. The salesperson neglected to tell us that the mattress that came with the $900 sofa bed was a pretend mattress, one you might endure only for one short night after partying very late! We had more regular use in mind. After waking up the first morning with a pair of those "stay with you past noon" backaches, we called to get an upgrade mattress. Our salesperson was not in on that Saturday morning and we were transferred to a manager. He turned out to be Mr. Rules "Я" Us.

139

"An upgrade mattress will cost you sixty dollars," he staunchly asserted, as though reciting the penalty for landing on his part of the Monopoly board. He also informed us that they would not be able to take back the mattress that came with the sofa or give us any credit. My blood temperature began to rise. This was the first product we had purchased from this relatively new store, and we were starting to feel our "change hit us in the back."

Several calls later, we finally got Mr. Rules to give us a thirty-dollar credit on what he called the "soiled" mattress, but we would have to bring it in ourselves, and there would be no delivery on the upgraded mattress. Mattresses do not fold or bend to be neatly transported in the back seat of a car.

We arranged for a friend with a truck, and a half day off, to pick up the old mattress at our lake house and take care of the exchange; the furniture company agreed to let us mail them a check for the difference. That same day, I mailed them a check for thirty dollars.

We never heard from our salesperson. There was no follow-up to see if the new mattress was satisfactory. Two weeks later we received a bill from the furniture company for a dollar fifty with a note from Mr. Rules: "You neglected to pay tax on the upgraded mattress. Please remit immediately so we can balance our books." My blood temperature hit the 212-degree point!

Partnerships are remembered positively because of what you give to them, not for what you take from them. Customer partnerships work best when the customer experiences service from providers willing to overlook imperfections in the math of the moment in exchange for the fairness of the future. Customers are particularly averse to service providers who wire their systems to their own strong advantage.

140

Quickly glance at our gas bill and tell me how much we owe Lone Star Gas:

◆ Lone Star Gas Company
PLEASE RETURN THIS PORTION WITH YOUR PAYMENT

MY CONTRIBUTION OF $_____ TO PROJECT HAP'N IS INCLUDED WITH MY PAYMENT.

SERVICE: (555) 781-7743
BILLING: (555) 781-7744   0613962   1273

DALLAS TX   27505   18063

DUE DATE FOR CURRENT BILL MO DAY YR	CAR–RT SORT	**CR 04
GROSS AMOUNT DUE AFTER THIS DATE 112293	BELL, CHIP R. 2 PARTNER WAY	
GROSS AMOUNT * $85.52	DALLAS TX 75678	
PROMPT PAYMENT AMOUNT NET AMOUNT $83.95		

If you said $85.52, you are like most people whom I have asked this question. This number is immediately beside the name and has an asterisk beside it. The correct amount, if you paid on time, is $83.95. When I contacted the gas company, the representative said, "Oh, don't worry. If you overpay, we'll credit it on your next bill." Did many people pay the wrong amount? "Mostly new customers; the older ones learn where to look," he informed me. Then the smart alack in me dropped one more line. "I hope you realize you have set it up so that I give you a free loan each time I fail to read the fine print." The bill was also set on a twenty-nine-day billing cycle; the typical customer pays bills every month. You can see where that leads you.

I am happy to announce that Lone Star Gas this very month changed the design of their bill. "The new bill format," according to David Millheiser, director of marketing for Lone Star Gas, "grew out of a move to focus on customer service. We, as did many members of our industry, let cost control and computer limitations dictate how we communicated with our customers. This new bill format is one of the first visible signs of our renewed customer focus and we are proud of the results."

141

Last week I took my clothes to the cleaners near my Dallas home. John was polite and responsive. "Boy, some of these customers can really ruin your day, you know?" he said as he counted my shirts. I noticed over my shoulder a man with an angry look putting his laundry in the back seat of his car. "Yeah, I guess so," I numbly answered.

"They seem to always want you to do 'em a favor," he continued, shaking his head in puzzlement.

I thought to myself how much I missed ol' Paul Langford and Heritage Cleaners.

❝ If you want to lift yourself up, lift up someone else. ❞

— Booker T. Washington

Chapter 18

PARTNERSHIP ELASTICITY

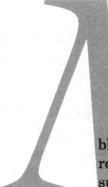ISS LENA HARTLEY, bless her heart, was wrong. And she really was trying to be helpful. But sure as rain, she was wrong.

When Nancy Marie Raincy of Walnut Ridge, Arkansas, gave a "yes" answer to my "Will you be my life partner?" question, it was one of the happiest days of my life. But getting married in the deep South in 1965 was not without challenges. In particular it meant getting the blessing of the guardians of local civility and protocol — the Women's Missionary Circle Number 4 of the First Baptist Church.

The setting for this important rite was a shower for my then bride-

143

to-be, sponsored by the circle. The fact that I was a marry-
ing an assertive, razor-sharp Arkansas girl imposed a
special inspection requirement on these ladies. Not only
was she from out of town, they weren't sure she was really
from the South. To a Northerner, this may sound pecu-
liar. Arkansas is not New Jersey — but it isn't Alabama-
Mississippi-Georgia-Tennessee either! So the shower
lasted a little longer than usual.

Boys were not invited to showers (the women in
the circle always referred to the opposite gender as "boys,"
no matter their age). The boys sat in their trucks and cars
in the church parking lot waiting to drive their wives,
girlfriends, moms, or brides-to-be home when the shower
finally ended. And of course, shower waiting had rituals
as rich as shower attending.

Grooms-to-be were allowed by the ladies of Circle
Number 4 to come into the social room only at the very
end of the shower — to help load up all the loot! There
was, however, an expectation that the male intruder would
give the appropriate oohs and ahs when cued with a
"Come look at this!" It was also the opportunity for one of
the senior ladies to pull the groom-to-be aside and render
the verdict of their bride-to-be inspection. Having talked
with some of the "ol' boys" during the shower-waiting
part, I had learned a bit about the ladies' special scoring
system.

The highest score you could get was "You don't
deserve her," usually pronounced after a stern "Boy!" and
a very long pause. That designation, however, was typically
reserved for a member of the high-school homecoming
court whose family's family's family had helped charter
the church. "Lovely" and "special" were sort of the next
best category. The barely passing grade was usually a
plural pronouncement like "I know you two will be very
happy." Miss Lena was the chosen pronouncer.

I was passing by the choir rehearsal room in the
church educational building on my way to the car with an
armful when she almost timidly pulled me aside. The look

on her face telegraphed her dilemma. This inspection was unique. My assertive, high-spirited, obviously very bright bride-to-be from out of town (and possibly out of the South) had defied their grading protocols.

"Be tolerant," she said. I was confused! Was this a grade the ol' boys had missed, a piece of advice, or a round-about way of admitting "We don't know how to grade what you've chosen — so go and be tolerant!'"? Then she added, "You'll do fine if you're just tolerant." Over the next thirty years, I learned that Miss Lena was "in the right church, but the wrong pew."

Partnerships need stretch, not tolerance

Miss Lena thought the best way to remain in a partnership with a high-spirited, mind-of-her-own partner was to be tolerant. But partnerships don't require tolerance. They require elasticity! And customer partnerships are no different.

Tolerance implies a kind of sufferance, an enduring resignation. It suggests the tone Mrs. Pope used in her fifth-grade class when she sighed her familiar and patronizing "We'll all wait until Chip decides to settle down and join the rest of us." Tolerance conveys endurance and fortitude. That's not the partnership way. Partnerships require give and flex; they expand to accommodate.

Tolerance-based relationships are exercises in long-suffering. There is a degree of rigidity about them. Such rigid relationships have the volume turned up on every flaw and error. People in relationships based on tolerance are perpetually pained by partner imperfections, but suffer in silence, in resignation: "This unfortunate disruption just comes with the territory."

Elasticity is about buoyancy, the opposite of rigidity. Elastic relationships have shock absorbers.

They expand and unfold in their acceptance; little bumps in the rocky road of partnership are absorbed without attention. It is the difference between a telephone pole and a willow.

Jack Russell Rainey was the King of Rural Mail Route Number 1 in Northeast Arkansas. Jack's letter-carrier route was one he took over after his father retired from the U.S. Post Office. Now if you were in the grocery store with Jack when he happened to encounter one of his "boxholders," as he called his customers, you would instantly spot a partnership based on two-way devotion.

Jack was also my wife's father. On one visit I asked Aunt Rachel about Jack's secret to mail magic. I knew she had spent many years listening to cheers from Jack's many fans. "He brags about their fudge," she explained, as if I would instantly catch the meaning and knowingly respond, "Oh, I see." Instead, I responded with puzzlement: "But Jack's allergic to chocolate."

"That's just the point," she said, pride resonating in her voice. "You see, Jack has a way of accepting his boxholders as they are — and adoring them as he finds them." Most folks might turn down an "I just baked you some fresh brownies" with a "Thanks, but I'm trying to watch my weight." Jack not only graciously took whatever they offered (there were others at Jack's house who loved chocolate), he asked for their recipe.

Now Jack wasn't just buttering up the lonely blue-haired widows who had little to do but crochet and cook. It was Jack's orientation in all relationships. When Jack was asked, "Where's a good place to fish?" he'd reveal his secret fishing hole on Black River. Despite his severe allergies to cat hair, he enjoyed (not endured) a forty-year continuous string of adopted kittens.

Partnerships are nurtured through resilience more than endurance

*C*ustomer partnerships are about affirming relationships more through ebb and flow than give and take. They encourage elbow room rather than close inspection. They seek ways to open rather than means to close. Instead of nitpicking details, partners roll with normal imperfections.

What does this imply for customer partnerships? Instead of recoiling at small glitches, try rolling with unexpected jabs with an expansive "Don't sweat the small stuff" orientation. When customers put too much energy into little details, surprise them by joyfully yielding on their too-loud demands. You may shock them and delight yourself!

Examine your business practices. Do you make customers go to the *n*th degree to get what they need? Are there barriers that make it difficult to get an unusual request fulfilled? Do service-delivery systems evoke necessary tolerance in your customers? Try calling someone in your unit; disguise your voice and ask for something unique or out of the ordinary. Do your associates expand, or do they recoil? Do they tell, or do they ask?

McGuffy's Restaurants, headquartered in Asheville, North Carolina, has a norm: "The answer is 'Yes,' what is the question?" This "We'll figure out a way to do whatever you need" attitude is a signal that assertive acceptance is more virtuous than stoic tolerance. It lets employees show the customer optimistic fluidity, not self-sacrificing indulgence.

Miss Lena was the epitome of tolerance. She was truly a devoted, sweet, gentle woman. I learned shortly after her death at over a hundred that her life philosophy was about endurance and tolerance. Perhaps her awkward pronouncement of the circle's verdict had more to say about her needs than my upcoming relationship adventure. That's okay, she gave it her best shot — and her heart was definitely devoted to my welfare.

Nancy Marie Rainey Bell is still the high-spirited, restless racehorse she was thirty years ago. Sharing a relationship with her has taught me that tolerance belongs only in relationships *without* spirit. Put tolerance in a vigorous relationship, and you have a recipe for iron-handed conflicts and energy wasted on minutiae.

Partnership elasticity, on the other hand, stretches the relationship so it can breathe and expand. And partners who flow together grow together.

> 66 *No person has a right to treat any other 'tolerantly,' for tolerance is the assumption of superiority.* 99
> — Wendell L. Willkie

GRACE

grace *n*. 1. Beauty or charm of form, composition, movement, or expression. 2. An attractive quality, feature, manner, etc.

Amazing Grace

The images of grace inspire
   both service giver and the buyer.
The Grand Canyon at setting sun,
   Joyner-Kersee on the run.

Autumn geese in V-shaped flight;
   Rembrandt art in morning light.
Mozart played on concert grands,
   the gentle clasp of infant hands.

Evening rain on old tin roofs;
   horses race on lightning hoofs.
Whitney's unique way with tunes,
   swans on rivers late in June.

Porsches' speed on steep-banked track;
   Michael Jordan's slam dunk knack.
Black limousines by Rolls Royce;
   the range of Pavarotti's voice.

Maui at the edge of dawn;
   fashion Ralph Lauren has sewn.
Hepburn's style with screenplay lines;
   both Ramses and the King Tut finds.

Partnerships will more than thrive
   when contributions come alive,
when graceful service takes the lead
   and elegantly meets a need.

Chapter 19

GRACEFUL PARTNERSHIPS

*I*T'S AGAINST OUR POLICY" has to be among the top ten show-stopping lines. It kills customer service, employee spirit, and partnerships.

In December, I was working near Washington, D.C., and stayed one night at a new hotel, one of a large chain I frequent about fifty nights a year. This particular property was at a location just far enough from the airport to make renting a car less expensive than taking a taxi.

Arriving at the hotel late and tired, I accidently left the inside dome light switched on in the rental car. The following morning I paid for my late-night error with a dead battery.

I walked the fifty feet from the parking lot to the hotel lobby. Warmly greeting the front-desk clerk with my very best "I need your help" voice, I explained my need for jumper cables plus someone with an auto to give the car battery a jump. "Let me call hotel engineering," he cheerfully responded. I was beginning to feel relieved and confident I would still be on time for my very important breakfast meeting five miles away.

I watched as he hung up the phone. His serious expression at least gave me some warning. "Engineering informed me that the hotel has a policy against assisting guests with dead batteries. You will have to call for a tow truck."

He let the words end with the punctuation of a slamming door. The sounds of Christmas music in the hotel lobby added a touch of irony to the tense scene. "Let me see if I have jumper cables," another guest said, attempting to rescue the situation. The front-desk clerk remained stolid, as if the engineer's pronouncement had turned him to salt.

Some minutes later, with my automobile finally running, I returned to the lobby. I had invested too much in this hotel chain to let this situation pass. It was a partnership I was not ready to end simply on the words of a grouchy basement employee on the other end of a phone. "What is the reason for the no-jumper-cable rule?" I asked.

The clerk barely looked at me as he delivered the facts. "The engineer told me that an employee in one of our hotels assisted a guest several years ago and the guest claimed it damaged his motor. He sued the hotel, and management put in the rule." Somehow the "bear trap" policy had captured his spirit just as it had my rescue.

But I was not finished with this issue. "What do *you* think?" I asked.

"Me? I don't know. I just work here." His IQ seemed to be dropping before my very eyes.

I persisted. "What would you have done if I had been your neighbor instead of a hotel guest?" I asked, still trying to find some humanity in a person who now seemed like an android.

There was a pause. Almost as if snapping out of a stupor, he stated the obvious: "Neighbors don't have policies!"

Partners aren't ruled by policies

Great customer partnerships are graceful. They make the experience of service one laced with ease and comfort. Graceful partnerships have a quiet, unencumbered elegance about them that makes the participant or spectator look back with awe. They are not bump-free, but they are shock-free.

There are countless definitions of grace, but the pervading concept in all is one of flow and polish. Music by Handel, movie performances by Jodie Foster, poetry by Browning, hotels by Four Seasons, cars by Mercedes, speed skating by Bonnie Blair — all display grace with confidence and ease.

Graceful customer partnerships have an "at home" feeling. Why do we like being home? Sure, there are often loved ones to affirm our presence and importance. But a large part of the comfort of home is its predictability: knowing where the extra paper towels are located, what to do with dirty clothes, when the morning paper will be delivered, what to do if the electric circuit blows. It is the familiarity that enables us to negotiate our entire dwelling in the dark of night, without bumps and bruises.

Customers honor service providers that endow the process of getting service with grace, ease, and predictability. When a bank promises "hassle-free" banking, it is making an offer with very little value added to most customers. Our orientation is that hassle-free should be the minimum price of admission in the service-providing game. Consumerships may be able to get away with a "hassle-free" standard; partnerships require much more.

Partnerships with grace are crafted around customer needs

*G*raceful partnerships base service-delivery systems on customers' critical success factors — their priorities for the service experience. Then they learn their customers' exact standards for those factors. They build into their data collection a way to perpetually update service standards and performance.

A major health-insurance company we were working with was about to shift to an "Answer the phone in three rings" standard when customer focus groups determined that phone access between 5 p.m. and 8 p.m. was significantly more important than top-speed phone answering. "Answering the phone in a hurry is nice," customers said, "But what's really important is not having to talk about really personal medical things in front of your friends at work."

Graceful service systems seek to eliminate even the smallest detractor in the customer's path. "Simple and predictable" means that customers get what they want without a lot of hassle, fanfare, or clutter. The legendary service providers take an "empathy walk;" they try to see their service-delivery system through their customers' eyes. Try to discover the potholes or blind alleys in your delivery system that may sidetrack customers as they seek to get their service needs met.

San Antonio–based USAA insurance and financial services sends customers only product information it knows relates to their situation and lifestyle. The company's computer looks up as many as 140 personal variables about each customer and matches the data against known buying profiles to predict likely purchasing trends based on life events such as moving, promotion, birth of a child, college expenses, and so forth. They practice well-honed approaches that leave the customer feeling cared for.

Service providers in pursuit of graceful service-delivery systems store information about customers' unique needs and requests. They train customer-contact people to be attentive to customers' special requirements and provide them a way to apply what they learn to the service-delivery system.

Graceful systems are crafted with an eye toward trust. Hardee's fast-food restaurant was among the first in its industry to let customers fill their own cups with ice and soft drinks. The savings in staff time and the increase in speed of service more than compensated for the occasional loss due to "excessive refills." The "make your own salad" bar was another fast-food innovation that had a similar goal. Embassy Suites Hotels gets high marks from patrons for its lobby self-serve breakfasts.

157

Graceful systems define easy access in the broadest manner possible. For instance, bank by mail is the traditional view; bank by electronic mail is the '90s view. What if hospitals eliminated universally applied visiting hours? Could you serve your customers better if you eliminated allegiance to hours, to location, to people? Would a drive-up make a difference? How would adding twenty-four-hour delivery service affect your customers' experience and perception? What if all your service people had beepers? Could customers easily reach you on a Sunday afternoon if necessary?

Graceful partnerships get partners to be a part

*P*artnership is about participation. Graceful systems get customers to help reinvent the service-delivery system. Customers often lack the historical blinders that service providers have. Since customers don't understand the reasons you can't do it, they can better see how it could be done. A customer-advisory team to assist in streamlining, simplifying, and expediting can be a boon to partnerships and graceful systems.

The heyday of "knock your socks off" service has of late yielded rich dividends to the devotees — and improved successes even to the "sorta sold." Customers now willingly pay more for great service. And today's customers tell pollsters that service in general is improving in most industries. Car buyers now care as much about the J. D. Power results on quality as they do the *Consumer Reports* rundown on value. Disposable is taking a back seat to dependable; value is revered over cost.

When today's hospital patients rate "how I was treated" as having a higher priority than "did I get well," you know the *end result* is a given, and the *process* for getting that result the key distinguisher. Today's service winners are the service providers who recognize that simply having a quality product or outcome is table stakes — the minimum price of admission into the game. The service game is won by superior memory-making processes — service full of grace.

❝*Beauty and grace command the world.*❞

— Park Benjamin

Chapter 20

PARTNERING UNDER PRESSURE

*T*HE FLIGHT OUT OF LAS VEGAS would be full; they always are on Sunday nights. As the taxi weaved through traffic, I realized that not only was I cutting it close on time, I had a reservation but no seat assignment. Without a seat, I was at risk of getting bumped. With a nervous quiver in my voice, I beseeched the driver to ask his radio dispatcher to call the airline and try to get me a seat assignment.

"Are you kidding me?" said the driver. "Our dispatcher services three cab companies and over five hundred cabs. She'll just laugh if I even ask." "Please just try it," I persisted. He did — in one of those "You won't believe what this guy in my cab is asking for" tones of voice. I was beginning to feel that I was barking up a very wrong tree.

But the dispatcher for Yellow-Checker-Star cab companies fooled us both. She responded to my desperate request with such great calmness and confidence, I would have thought she got several hundred such requests a week. After a brief pause, she gave me an assignment. "I need the passenger's help," she typed on the taxicab computer. "Please give me destination, flight number, and the airline's phone number if you have it." I wheeled into action with all the requested information.

Time passed as we sped toward McCarran International. In a few minutes a message appeared on the cab driver's computer monitor: "The airline has put me on hold, will advise." I was starting to be very impressed and assured that a pro was on my case. A minute later, the message came back, "Too late to get a seat, the airline says the flight has been delayed and you should be just fine. Good luck. Hope you make it all right!"

"This is amazing," mumbled the driver, overwhelmed by the dispatcher's tenacity and determination. I asked the driver for the dispatcher's name. Thank you, Rebecca Thomas! You made a hectic business trip to Las Vegas end on a very positive note by partnering with me under extraordinary pressure.

We live in a world in which customers are demanding faster, more convenient access. The advent of "We will shop for you" services, Domino's speedy pizza delivery, Jiffy Lube, catalog shopping, automated teller machines, all stand as evidence that fast is favored and easy is expected. The underside of this "service under fire" requirement is that it makes the service provider struggle to provide quality at a reasonable price while delivering it all in a hurry.

Four principles may help you provide great service partnerships under pressure. I call them the "Becky Thomas approach" to nervous service. You may have others that have worked for you.

Look for ways to foster customer activity

*G*iving the customer something to do enfolds him in the effort and moderates his impatience. Just as Disney manages long lines by entertaining guests with music, movies, and Disney characters while they wait, look for ways to foster customer activity.

I broke my finger some time ago while consulting out of town. I asked my client to stop by the nearest hospital emergency room on our way to dinner so I could have my finger x-rayed and, if needed, set in a splint. The long wait in the emergency room began to wear on my patience and (I worried) my client's — a quick trip was turning into an evening-long affair. When it was finally my turn, the nurse sensed my impatience and asked if I was in a hurry. I explained my situation.

"We're swamped tonight," she said pleasantly, "But I can get you out of here quickly if you can do a few chores for me." I cheerfully delivered my chart for her, took a trip to the pharmacy to get splints, and escorted myself to x-ray. The night was shorter, I got out quicker, and probably so did she.

Remember to let your customers see you pause before giving assignments. It is important for customers to know you gave thoughtful consideration to an appropriate assignment. Becky did not snap back a quick "Do this and I will help you." Consider what the customer is able to do, might prefer to do, needs to do to make the service more expedient.

Don't tell the customer your problems

*C*ustomers are driven by their needs, especially under pressure. As selfish as that may sound, customers are far more interested in getting what they want than in hearing about your troubles. It's your job to meet their needs, not theirs to cheer you up. Nervous service customers hear a "how bad it is" response and think, "Just tell me yes or no. Don't lay a guilt trip on me now." The behind-the-scenes hassles you must negotiate are not their concern. The service person who tells hard-luck stories quickly frustrates customers and drives them to other service providers who will cheerfully respond to their request or tactfully say, "I would very much like to do that for you. However, I cannot at this time. What I *can* do for you is . . . ," or "What I would recommend is that you. . . ."

Stay focused, but visibly responsive and pleasant

*E*ver watch a duck moving upstream in a creek? It appears to be gliding smoothly across the water, serene and confident. Under the surface, though, the duck is paddling frantically against the current. The service provider who is working diligently to deliver nervous service must maintain a visible aura of confidence. She must also communicate focus and attention to the customer. If response to a customer query is delayed for reasons beyond your control, keep your reasons buried — ". . . as soon as I have a free phone line I will. . . ."

"Front-line frantic" communicates fear to the customer. Acting with urgency is appropriate; acting with panic and frenzy is not. A part of demonstrating focus is to actively keep the customer updated on your progress. Customers become more anxious faced with the unknown than with the unpleasant and known. Time passing with no sign of progress is a big unknown in the customer's mind.

Seek happy endings

*L*et the customer know you were honored to serve her, even under difficult circumstances. Try to build a tie to future service. "I look forward to the next time we get to serve you. Maybe it will be under less hectic circumstances and we can show you what we *really* can do!" Remember that the last encounter with your customer will likely be the one remembered and described to others.

Anyone can serve well — on a slow day. Only the best can be good under fire. "Nervous service" with distinction communicates confidence to customers. It is a "When the going gets tough, the tough get going" message that telegraphs reliability — and reliability helps partnerships develop the strength to endure and flourish.

163

" *Progress flows only from struggle.* "

— Louis Brandeis

Chapter 21

PARTNERING IN AN EMERGENCY

I WAS A 1989 HURRICANE HUGO victim! Fortunately, I was one of the lucky ones: at least I wasn't forced to sport a lapel button that read "Don't mess with me, I STILL don't have power!" a week after the storm. But I was forced to spend hours with a chain saw, cleaning up my back yard. As a result, I neglected the close client encounters I try to practice. I am quite sure certain clients heard the strain in my voice when they called with unique service requests.

As a service-quality consultant, I am perpetually challenged to practice what I preach. When I found myself caught in this frustrating emergency, I became curious about other service providers who struggle to maintain high service standards in the face of an unexpected service breakdown. How do they do it?

To find out, I interviewed a few "service winners" — companies we mention in the same sentence with service excellence. I also practiced closer-than-usual observation of the local "best" at their worst. There was amazing consistency in their adherence to several principles. It's no accident that these organizations maintain a reputation for pleasing customers, despite the pain of an emergency.

With obvious honesty, lower customer expectations

*A*t Four Seasons Hotels, new front-desk clerks wear name badges with "trainee" under the clerk's name. Management finds that it encourages guests to be less demanding and more forgiving of mistakes. It also enables novices to take more risks as they transform shaky skills into confident mastery. In a similar manner the emergency, if honestly addressed, can prepare customers for less service quality than they might normally expect.

Vision Cable of North Carolina (Charlotte) was hit hard by Hurricane Hugo. But the company, known for its excellent service, did everything it could to keep customers informed. It ran radio ads in which the general manager explained the situation this way:

> As you know, many of our customers have been hard hit by Hurricane Hugo, and so was Vision Cable. Miles of cable have been destroyed and thousands of hookups to homes have been knocked down. Vision Cable has restored service to more than one-half of the service area. We are still continuing our night-and-day effort to restore service to 100 percent of our customers. We sincerely appreciate your patience. You

can help us by only calling our office to report individual service lines to your home which are down. Please be assured that adjustments will be made on your November bill for the period you were without service. For those customers whose service has already been restored, you may still experience an occasional interruption as construction crews for the power company and Vision Cable make additional repairs. Should an interruption last longer than one-half hour, please do call our office to report the address and the time of the interruption. Again, thank you for your patience during this effort.

After the emergency was over, the general manager explained the company's service philosophy to me: "We try to treat all our customers *like neighbors*. We believe if you are honest and straightforward with customers, they will treat *you* like a neighbor when circumstances beyond your control put you in a 'one-down' position."

167

Fix the customer, then the customer's problem

A major snowstorm stranded airplanes in Richmond. Passengers grew more and more irritated as they discovered they would be remaining overnight in the wrong city *and* all nearby hotels were filled to capacity. As gate attendants struggled with the long lines to make early morning flight reservations, Delta Airlines had flight attendants serve passengers from the stock previously loaded on the now-grounded aircraft. Hot coffee, warm blankets, milk for infants, snacks, playing cards, and magazines were quickly transferred from plane to terminal. Passengers were mollified or at least could see Delta was doing everything it could to make them as comfortable as possible.

Customer research for a major telephone company turned up a discrepancy between customer expectations and actual practice that demonstrates the same principle. When the telephone repair technicians arrived at a residence to restore service, they invariably began their requested repair work by going to the side of the customer's house or up a nearby pole. Yet customer interviews and surveys strongly indicated that customers expected the repair person first to knock on the front door like a neighbor to announce his or her presence and intention. "After all," customers said, "the phone company *did* require me to take the day off to be there for the phone to be repaired." Fix the customer, then fix the customer's service problem.

168 Focus on partnership, not end-usership

*H*ugo resulted in an unexpected overload at Myers Park Hardware in Charlotte as customers rushed to purchase candles, propane gas, camping stoves, flashlight batteries, and other emergency supplies. The store turned to its patrons for help. As three frequent customers were recruited by the store manager to assist in bagging merchandise and ringing up sales, the crowd of formerly frustrated customers suddenly broke out in applause. These "volunteers" also registered their pleasure with the scene by offering to give up their "helper" slot to the highest bidder. It became a bit like Tom Sawyer convincing his skeptical onlookers that whitewashing a fence was an honor for only the carefully chosen and lucky few!

Give the customer honesty; plead for customer patience

A Southwest Airlines flight from Dallas to Houston was loaded and ready to depart when airline maintenance noticed that the signal light for the windshield heater was not working properly. The pilot's explanation for the delay got very technical; he talked to the passengers as if they were all aeronautical engineers. Yet his customers appeared relieved and settled in for a lengthy delay. "I don't know what he said," commented one passenger, "but he sounds like he knows what he's doing."

At moments of service anxiety and instability, customers need demonstrations of confidence and competence from service providers. This is one reason front-line empowerment is important. Give more details, not fewer; data overload (normally a negative) can bolster customers' confidence by assuring them they are in good hands.

169

Create a "This is very unusual" perspective

A lthough I had a guaranteed reservation at a Marriott Hotel in Boston, I found "no room at the inn" when I arrived very late one evening. The hotel's recovery response was impressive, but I still had to sleep in another hotel some distance away. The following week I again arrived late at the Marriott and the same front-desk manager, Jan Blum, was about to "walk" me again. An earlier power outage nearby had forced several hotels to divert their arriving guests to the Marriott, which did have power. Realizing my past patience would likely turn into ire if I were bumped again, Blum said with a twinkle in his eye, "I have a surprise for you! We never use Room 500 in overbooked situations like this. But you are a special guest, it's very late, and you are only here for one evening. I want you to get Room 500. I will be on duty in the morning as you check out, and I'll be very anxious to get your reaction to this unusual room!"

Even the bellman looked surprised as I handed him my luggage and the key to Room 500. The mystery room turned out to be a gigantic, two-bedroom penthouse suite with a panoramic view of Boston harbor, a sunken living room with fireplace, grand piano, library — the works! I immediately regretted that it was midnight and I was staying for only one evening. However, I would *never* expect such a delightful offer to occur again. Jan had carefully and sincerely positioned his heroic gesture as a "once in a lifetime" unique occurrence, not a normal scenario.

These five principles can be practical guidance for escaping emergencies with an excellent evaluation from customers. But it is important to remember that perceived culpability can play an important part in the customer's expectations during service-quality deterioration or breakdown. If the flight is late departing because a flight attendant failed to arrive on time, the airline may get little customer sympathy. However, if customers perceive the "less than expected" service to be due to a situation beyond the control of the service provider, they will be more reluctant to register low marks on their mental service report cards.

The service provider that considers itself "off the hook" simply by providing heroic service only during an emergency, however, is asking for trouble. Customers are more forgiving if service providers work as hard when things go wrong as they do to make service distinctive in normal times. The superstars of service all understand that unless extraordinary service actions accompany unusual emergency times, patrons will silently register their disappointment by taking their service business elsewhere.

171

❝ *A problem is a chance for you to do your best.* ❞

— Duke Ellington

PARTNERING WITH EMPLOYEES

Partnering with Employees

One of the most crucial partnerships in the service world is the one that occurs between supervisor and employee. Dr. Benjamin Schneider did a major research study at the University of Maryland to ascertain the factors that have the most impact on the quality of service to customers. His research concluded that the number-one variable affecting the quality of customer relations was the quality of employee relations.

John Longstreet of Harvey Hotels reminded us that his primary job was to make people feel good about serving guests. Bill Marriott, CEO of Marriott Corporation, said, "My job is to motivate them, teach them, help them, support them, and care about them. If we take care of them, they'll take care of the guests." One great leader after another communicates the same message: Great service to the customer begins with great service to those who serve the customer.

This section examines several of the key aspects of creating a partnership between service leader and service follower. The power difference poses a unique challenge in a relationship laced with opposing elements of control and freedom, dependence and independence, sovereignty and self-direction. Paradigms of the past often haunt leaders seeking to trade their dominance orientation for a more supportive posture. "New leaders" often struggle in their efforts to truly serve employees when they live within an organizational culture that values "The buck stops here" accountability and authority-driven influence.

Chapter 22

SERVING AS LEADER: ROLES

I WENT TO *Roget's Thesaurus* for inspiration. I'd not really looked at *Roget's* since trying to write a term paper for Mrs. Ridley's twelfth-grade English composition class! "What message would I get," I wondered, "If I looked up 'service' and thought about leadership." I was surprised at how much I learned.

The word "service" has many meanings. It might mean "assistance" or "help," as in "We are here to be of service." But the word can also mean "duty," as in "Were you in the service?" It can imply "ceremony," as in "We went to the eleven o'clock service." And finally, it can suggest "maintenance," as in "I took my car in for its ten-thousand-mile service." I skipped over references to amorous bulls, servitude, and silver eating utensils! But these four meanings — assistance, duty, ceremony, and maintenance — describe the role of the service leader.

Assistance: The leader as helper

*S*ervice leadership in the past meant control and consistency. The "boss" of yesteryear kept a tight rein, fearing that otherwise employees would get lazy and fail to work. We now are learning that employees act like adults when treated like adults. Employees who manage tight family budgets, buy and sell real estate, prepare complex tax returns, and juggle dental appointments with soccer games and ballet lessons probably have the wisdom and maturity to handle almost any work assignment. No one at home ensures they have empowerment or "appropriate supervision." No one at home completes their annual performance appraisal to ensure they get "an accurate assessment of their efforts and deficiencies." Yet they manage the roles of parent and spouse and citizen just fine, thank you very much!

The service leader's role is to support and serve employees. That means running interference and getting employees the resources they need to work effectively. It means planning, blazing new trails, and creating ways to be more effective as a team. It means treating employees as a very important customer segment and finding ways to meet their needs.

But who's in charge of control and consistency? As service leader, you still are! However, it is now something you pursue *with* employees, not something you *lay on* them. If employees are clear on organization and team goals, if they know the reasons why, and if they know the real (and appropriate) boundaries, they will *help* you ensure control and consistency if allowed. Look for ways to involve, include, and invite.

Duty: The leader as role model

*W*hen I was a new infantry officer about to assume my first combat assignment in Viet Nam, I asked the first sergeant what he thought my most important job was if I wanted to be a good officer. He didn't hesitate. "Be a good soldier," he said. It was his way of saying I needed to make sure my actions were always consistent with what I was asking the troops to be and do. It is the leader's first duty to honor a set of values through congruent actions.

177

Employees watch your moves, not your mouth. Cowboy humorist Will Rogers said it better: "People learn more from *observation* than from *conversation*." If you are telling employees that service is really important, are you personally demonstrating that priority through what you do? Effective leaders learn to be clear about their values and to seek every day to live professional lives that are consistent with those values, especially in moments of tough choices. If your employees watched where you put your energy for one week, what would they conclude is your top priority? Is that priority the legacy you would hope to leave your organization?

Ceremony: The leader as cheerleader

A few years ago one of my partners and I consulted with a successful reinsurance company whose average nonsupervisory professional employee, we were told, was twenty-seven years old and earned about $85,000 a year. Most were highly driven, Ivy League college–educated go-getters. Yet an employee-attitude survey revealed that they regarded themselves as under-rewarded. We first thought we were dealing with a bunch of spoiled brats who had no idea how the real world worked or that only a tiny fraction of the world's population made that kind of money, especially at that age. But we were wrong. "We know we are very well compensated," they told me. "We just don't feel valued and recognized for what we do!" Psychologist William James wrote, "The deepest principle of human nature is the craving to be appreciated."

Effective service leaders celebrate. Not the perfunctory retirement dinner or perfect-attendance ceremony — that's fine, but it's not enough. Great leaders look for occasions to publicly affirm excellence. They look for opportunities to tell stories of what they want others to model and emulate. They know that "celebration" begins with "see."

Maintenance: The leader as mentor

*G*reat service leaders know that quality improvement is continuous and that learning is never over. They know that if they want a climate of creativity and growth, they must honor learning and teaching. "He who is not busy being born is busy dying," Bob Dylan wrote in one of his folk songs. It is also true of organizations. As the world of service quality continues to change and get more complex, it is crucial that the service leader act as a mentor — always helping others learn and improve. Just as machines need proper maintenance to go the distance, so do people. In the organizational world, people maintenance involves increased competence and wisdom.

What does great service leadership entail? It means remembering that employees are your most important customers. They will give customers the quality of service they receive from their leaders. It means always ensuring that your actions are in sync with the actions employees are expected to perform. The values you live are the values they believe you honor. It means finding ways to inspire by making work inspirational. And it means helping employees learn, especially when they make errors.

The decade ahead will require even more focus on the customer than the past decade. The winning organizations will be those with great leaders, not efficient administrators. Successful leaders will be those willing to turn the organizational pyramid upside down and work daily to serve those who serve the customer. Be a responsive helper in your *assistance* role, a valued role model in your *duty* role, an inspirational cheerleader in your *ceremony* role, and a caring mentor in your *maintenance* role.

179

❝ *The great leader is seen as servant first, and that simple fact is the key to his greatness.* ❞
— Robert K. Greenleaf

Chapter 23

SERVING AS LEADER: GIFTS

I

N HIS BOOK *Leadership Is an Art,* Max De Pree wrote, "The first responsibility of the leader is to define reality (vision/dreams). The last role is to say 'thank you.' In between the two, the leader must become a servant."

Max's simplicity and his focus on leaders as visionaries and inspirers are compelling. Leaders are also Vendors. A major part of leadership is providing supplies for those who serve the customer. It is a superordinate role — the kind captured in Scandinavian Airlines Systems CEO Jan Carlzon's oft-repeated "If you aren't serving the customer, your job is to be serving someone who is."

You may have noticed that I have capitalized Vendor. Leaders are super-Vendors. They are not go-fors. They partner with employees to provide special supplies or leadership gifts. A leader is the sole-source Vendor for some of the supplies needed for employees to partner effectively with customers.

Six special gifts

What are the special gifts or supplies that are given by leaders? What are some of the ways leaders partner with employees?

Focus

Focus is how the leader communicates the rationale for work effort. It is embodied in concepts like purpose, aim, dreams, vision, mission, and direction. Focus lies not only in having a purpose, but in leading and living consistent with that purpose.

Brookfield Development is a large construction/property-management company. It builds and manages large office complexes. The Ontario Division has a very clear purpose: "Our tenants are our partners. We will be successful only if they are successful. We make their work world safe and comfortable by anticipating and responding to their needs."

John Campbell is the leader of the Ontario Division. He supplies his employees *focus* by anticipating and responding to their unique needs. "They will partner with tenants only as well as I partner with them," he says. He visits tenants almost daily, enthusiastically championing to them his special Brookfield team. Regular all-manager meetings are held to "revisit the vision and renew the focus." Most meetings include a success story or two about how a team member partnered with a tenant in a way that helped bring greater success to the tenant.

Family

Family is the manner the leader uses to create and encourage a context for kinship and "forum." It is carried out in the gatherings the leader sponsors. It is the basis of teamwork and collaboration.

Family does not mean leader as parent, employees as children. It means encouraging respect, caring, and unconditional positive regard. Members of a healthy, fully functioning family feel jointly responsible to one another, know how to trade on one another's strengths, and are committed to collective success. Their interdependent actions give customers confidence; their mutual commitments show customers a sense of joy.

183

Howard Leibowitz is vice president and director of engineering and operations planning for Nabisco Foods' Biscuit Division. While his management team members represent very diverse areas, they regularly meet to build support and teamwork. Team norms such as "The people who come to the team meeting are the right people" help the team learn to rely on the wisdom of the group rather than depend on any single member who may not be present. Team meetings are critiqued before adjournment to foster a never-ending effort to improve the "family council." Periodically, the team devotes time to team building (or enhancement) to improve working relationships and ensure collective focus.

Freedom

Freedom has to do with the many ways in which leaders allow, encourage, and support initiative among employ-

ees. It does not mean unlimited license. It deals with
the degree to which the leader is willing to share control
with employees. It is the recognition that empowerment
(our current phrase for freedom) is not a gift. The leadership goal is liberation — eliminating the obstacles (no
purpose, no protection, no permission, no proficiency)
that inhibit employees from demonstrating responsible
freedom.

Sharon Decker, whom you met in chapter 12, is
widely known for her employee-esteem-building efforts.
"We hire good people, provide them good training, give
them good coaching, and get out of their way so they can
make good judgments," she says. "When you raise children, the more mature they get, the more freedom they
get. We *start off* with mature people. The amount of freedom they get tells them how adult we think they are.
My everyday job is to remind our customer-service people
by my trust just how adult I think they are."

184

Flow

Flow is what the leader supplies to enable employees to
stay the course — on their own power. Think of a river of
human energy. Leaders supply assistance to keep the flow
at the optimum level. It involves helping employees have
clear expectations and direction. It involves letting go of
improper control so that the flow is not constricted or
subject to rebellious reaction on the part of employees.
Balanced control yields current without rapids and guiding banks without disruptive twists and turns.

The leader partners with employees by running
interference, anticipating obstacles, and finding ways to
eliminate them before they disrupt. Leaders enhance flow
by providing opportunities for perpetual growth and
continuous competence. Such leaders help ensure that
work expectations and priorities are clear and realistic.
They make certain that employees are always supplied

with the tools, time, and resources they need to partner with customers.

Forgiveness

Forgiveness is about openness and vulnerability. It is in part the ability to admit mistakes and express feelings. It encompasses the self-forgiveness that enables leaders to demonstrate openness and honesty, as well as the other-forgiveness that lets them meet employee mistakes with mentoring rather than rebuke. It is the key ingredient and attitude needed for true growth and mature risk taking. Nicholas Imparato and Oren Harari argue that in an environment that fosters innovation and customer partnership, imperfections and human errors will inevitably occur. The organization that creates a climate of "problem analysis rather than blame analysis" instills the confidence in its people to continue appropriate risk taking.

185

Fun/faith

Fun/faith is the spirited side of leadership that fosters a sense of joy. It is the part of the leader that encourages celebration and lightness. It is the security to seek the humanity in work. It is taking one's purpose seriously while not taking oneself seriously. It is the ability to be quick to praise and always in pursuit of good endings. It is radiating joy that propels employees to "keep on keeping on." It gives them the faith to withstand difficulties and not give up.

Martin Broadwell, a training consultant in Atlanta, describes the affirmation that results from fun and faith as a bulletproof vest. "When customer-contact people encounter difficult and irate customers, their bulletproof vests will enable them to weather the situation without their morale fading." Edwin Thomas, CEO of Asbury

Methodist Village, a large, continuing-care retirement community in Gaithersburg, Maryland, said, "We added 'We will celebrate our successes' to our corporate values when we saw the power that having fun had on our resilience to provide consistently high-quality service to our residents and their families."

"Vendor" with a capital V has a different meaning than "vendor" spelled in lower case. The supplies leaders provide employees are critical to employees' ability to partner with customers. These supplies also help level the playing field between leader and follower. They help raise subordinate to the level of partner. Be a Vendor to your employees and watch them grow!

❝ *When the best leader's work is done the people say, 'We did it ourselves'.* ❞

— Lao-tsu

WITH
A LITTLE HELP
FROM
MY PARTNERS

... Well, Actually, More Than a Little

There was a point early in the writing of this book when I suddenly felt a little foolish. Here I was writing a book about partnership — by myself! I was reminded of many of the other paradoxes I had witnessed in my career, such as giving a lecture on participative learning or writing an empowerment policy.

I discussed this with one of my partners. He said that I was making more of the issue than was necessary. Coauthorship was not the only solution. He suggested that I invite each of my main partners to contribute a short chapter. In this way I could still solo the book while un-oxymoroning (I made that up!) the dilemma. What you are about to read is the result.

Ron Zemke *is president of* Performance Research Associates, *a consulting firm headquartered in Minneapolis that he started in 1972. He and I have been friends for twenty years, business partners for the last eight. Ron is the author of hundreds of articles and numerous books, including three bestselling classics:* Service America!, The Service Edge, *and* Figuring Things Out. *Ron and I coauthored* Service Wisdom *and* Managing Knock Your Socks Off Service. *He also coauthored* Delivering Knock Your Socks Off Service *and* Knock Your Socks Off Answers *(with Kristin Anderson) and* Sustaining Knock Your Socks Off Service *(with Tom Connellan). Ron lives near Minneapolis with his life partner, Susan Zemke.*

Dr. Thomas K. Connellan *manages the Ann Arbor, Michigan, office of* Performance Research Associates. *Tom was formerly associated with the University* *of Michigan's Executive Education Program. He is the author of five books, including* How to Grow People into Self Starters *and his most recent book,* Sustaining Knock Your Socks Off Service *(with Ron Zemke). Tom lives in Ann Arbor with his life partner, Dr. Pamela Dodd.*

Kristin Anderson *is a partner in the Minneapolis office of Performance Research Associates. She is the author of* Great Customer Service on the Telephone *and coauthor (with Ron Zemke) of* Delivering Knock Your Socks Off Service *and* Knock Your Socks Off Answers. *Kristin recently completed a series of training films based on her books and starring Lily Tomlin.*

Karen A. Revill *is an associate in the Ann Arbor office of Performance Research Associates. This is her first opportunity to have her work published. She lives near Ann Arbor with her partner, Troy Revill.*

Dr. Nancy R. Bell *just completed her law degree from Southern Methodist University in Dallas. Before entering law school in 1992, she spent twenty-six years in public education, the last ten as a school principal. She left her position as a high-school principal in North Carolina to pursue a new career in law. We have been life partners for over thirty years.*

Be prepared for varied styles and approaches in the chapters that follow. However, you should find a consistent theme: Customer dazzlement is a great goal toward which to shoot, but customer partnership is the important standard.

Chapter 24

RAIN AND SNOW AND DARK OF NIGHT KEEP THIS PARTNERSHIP ON COURSE

by Ron Zemke

LATE THANKSGIVING EVE Jeff Amland called. "I've been listening to the weather forecasts all day," he began, "and it sounds like there's gonna be three to six inches of snow on the ground by morning. Is there any specific time you need your driveway open tomorrow?"

There wasn't.

He persisted: "Don't you have out-of-town people coming?"

They'd already arrived and, since we'd been hearing the same weather predictions as Jeff, all had planned accordingly. We weren't going anywhere but down the lane and back, and that on foot, or at our most ambitious, on cross-country skis.

"Well, I'll put you down for afternoon then. But if you change your mind, call me at the shop. I'll be working on the plows for another couple of hours anyway."

Thanksgiving morning around eleven o'clock, Jeff called again. "I'll have you plowed out by three if that's still okay." We'd already been out on foot, and even though the village plow had thrown a couple of feet across the mouth of the drive, we could easily ram our way out to the highway in an emergency.

"Let me give you the number for the truck phone just in case."

Two years earlier less three days, we had hired Jeff, a.k.a. AAgro-GREEN Professional Lawn Services, to come plow us out from under a freak twenty-inch Thanksgiving snowstorm — the second such storm of the year. It was an act of blind desperation. Our regular snow-plowing guy had gone on vacation, and at 6:00 p.m. Thanksgiving day plus one, his designated emergency backup was impatiently explaining to me that he had a family he hadn't seen since 4:00 a.m. the previous day. Didn't I think, he bleated, that he and his deserved to celebrate the holiday weekend too? We gave him two hours to change his mind. He didn't. We called Jeff.

We didn't know Jeff from a post, as we say here in the Upper Midwest. But Jeff's flyer had been there in the accordion file we use for household bills and receipts, supermarket coupons, car and boat titles, canceled checks, and appliance warranties. We kept his mailbox stuffer for no clear reason other than "just in case."

"I have your snow-removal brochure. I know you're probably swamped, but we have a family member with a medical condition, we have relatives we're going to have to get to the airport tomorrow, and I can't find anyone willing to plow us out in less than two days."

"Has the village cleared the main road yet?"

It had — leaving a six-foot wall of ice and snow at the bottom of the hill in the process.

"Have you marked the sides?" I had, with four-foot orange stakes.

"Are you lit at night?" We are and were.

"I have two regular customers between where I am right now and where you are. So would 8:30 be soon enough?"

By 9:15 that evening we had a clear path to the main road and the relieved feeling that we could deliver our charges to the airport the next morning safely and on time. And AAgro-GREEN had a new customer.

That all transpired in November 1991. Mid-April of 1992, generally the end of the snowfall season here in Minnesota, Jeff stopped by with a bottle of wine. "Just a little thank-you for your business and for recommending me to so many of your neighbors." We had, gladly, and with no prompting.

"Did you get my note about maybe doing your lawn work this year?"

Jeff's "note" was a detailed assessment of the condition of our lawn — as much as the thaw had exposed, anyway — and a proposal for remedying the same; the dates he thought it should be thatched and fertilized and reseeded; the materials he felt would be appropriate to the job; and what he thought a reasonable mowing, edging, and weed-treatment schedule might look like. He also included information on how he would pick a start date and what he would do to put the lawn to bed in the fall. And the price, while not the lowest we'd ever seen on an estimate, was well within the competitive range.

Over the past two winters and summers, we've actually seen Jeff and crew working on our place only eight or ten times. In winter he plows after we've left — our arrangement, except for those rare occasions when nature visits us with a foot or more of snow in twenty-four hours — and in summer he mows and fertilizes and sprays the dandelion crop and fights the crabgrass before we're back home in the evening.

But we always know he's been there from the work — and from the notes. When he fertilizes or sprays, he leaves a note detailing the chemicals and whatnot he's used, along with a suggested watering schedule for the next few days. Last winter he clipped the top off an ornamental driveway light. The note recounted the damage — damage I would not have found on my own until spring, if at all — and asked me if there was some place special I'd like him to purchase the replacement, and to leave any special instructions for the reinstallation.

When Jeff adds a new person to his lawn-care or snow-removal crews, he brings him around in the evening and introduces him. "I'd hate for you to come home some day and find a stranger working on your property," he explains.

Then there are the little "dazzlements" — things he does just because he thinks they need doing and because "I just thought you might get a kick out of it." One evening last winter we arrived home unusually early and caught Jeff in the act of finishing up the driveway. Badly in need of a little fresh air and exercise, Susan and I did the walks and the upper apron of the driveway, while Jeff concentrated on de-icing the slippery crest of our thirty-degree drive. When the bill for that day arrived, he had deducted ten dollars from the usual total for, in his words, "removal assistance."

Last fall the warm weather lingered an unusually long time, and as a consequence leaf removal in the neighborhood moved at a rather leisurely pace. Particularly in our yard. When the weather took a sudden turn to the more normal — that is, became bitterly cold and blustery — Jeff rounded up a crew and canvassed his accounts, removing leaves where they had been allowed to languish and even moving lawn furniture to shelter for those of us who were irrationally holding out hope against hope for one more weekend of fun in the fall sun. And of course, none of that work ever appeared on an invoice.

I've talked with Jeff several times about his approach to his business — how he markets, how he decides to do what he does for his customers unbidden — and I've always learned a lot from him and a lot about how at least one customer-focused small-business owner's mind works. Paraphrasing our conversations — and doing a little interpretive tap dancing to fill in the holes — I think it's fair to say there are four keys to Jeff's approach to his business and his philosophy of partnering with his customers (though I dare say he might never choose these exact words or many of the preceding to express it.)

◆ As long as snow falls and grass grows in Minnesota, there will be a market for the grooming, management, and removal of both.

◆ People short on time and long on property are always in need of help in the maintenance and upkeep of that property. Particularly in regard to the boring stuff — like snow removal and grass cutting and a dozen or so other activities that lose their luster when in need of overly frequent repetition.

195

◆ As long as you move the snow out of the way on a regular, predictable basis, keep the grass short and green, and do the whole thing without worrying or inconveniencing the property owner, you'll have satisfied customers. And satisfied customers stay with you as long as nothing better — or seemingly better — comes along and lures them away.

◆ As long as you respect the property you work on, the wants and ways of the people you work for, and think about what you're doing — really think about, not just go through the motions, but think about the business you're in and the customers you want and the customers you have — it's going to stay interesting and a challenge.

Now, if Jeff ever heard me talking like this he would have a cow. To a reporter who asked me about memorable service I'd experienced, I once mentioned something Jeff had done — and he stammered for two days when he saw his name in the paper.

Nonetheless, Jeff knows — whether by intuition or from trial-and-error experience — two important things. The first is the value of keeping a customer, if not for life, for a long, long time. The second is that keeping customers for a long, long time means never taking them for granted and never believing that there isn't yet another interesting way to let your actions tell your customers you care about their business.

Chapter 25

PARTNERS CARE

by Tom Connellan

I

T WASN'T EASY PARKING a 1957 Buick Roadmaster in a space designed for 1993-sized cars. In the words of my daughter, the Buick was "a boat."

A boat it was, but it was my Aunt Dot's car nonetheless. And since Aunt Dot had broken her leg, she needed someone to drive her around. Today was my turn.

"There's a space right there, Tommy," she pointed out. Once I had reached the age of forty, I had thought she might switch to Tom. Or perhaps "Your Majesty." But Tommy I was, and Tommy I'll be.

So into the space I eased, with barely enough room to open the doors.

As we walked into the lobby of the post office, we maneuvered a gauntlet of "Hi's," "That must be her nephew from up North," and "How's the leg doing?"

Aunt Dot acknowledged each of the greetings in her own unique way — sort of like your aunt probably does. It's "her way." You can't really describe it — but you know it when you see it.

Eyeing the long line of white-haired heads leading up to the counter, each with a handful of letters, I calculated a twelve-to-fifteen-minute wait.

"Ummm, Aunt Dot, how many stamps do you need?"

Carefully counting the envelopes clutched in her right hand, she came back with a spry "Eight!"

"Well, I have an idea. We can get that many, and even more if we need them, from that stamp machine right over there."

Aunt Dot eyed the machine coldly.

"Yes," she replied imperiously, "but the machine won't ask me how my leg is!"

And that was the end of the discussion. But not the end of the lesson.

As I reflected on Aunt Dot's statement over the next twenty-one minutes, the profound impact of it on partnering with customers grew on me. Too often, we don't ask.

We ask other partners. "How was your day?" "What was the traffic like?" and "How did the presentation go?" are all common questions partners in marriages and committed relationships ask each other.

"What was hell week like?" "How did you make out on the French test?" and "Did you have fun at the dance?" are all questions for our college-student partners.

We ask those questions because we care. Because those partners are important to us.

Too often, however, customers are asked, "Howyadoin" in a manner that elicits a perfunctory "Fine" or even suggests that no answer is desired.

So as we approached the counter, and as my fifteen-minute estimate stretched into twenty-one minutes, I was curious as to how the interaction between Aunt Dot and the counter person was going to play out.

"Well, Dorothy, how *are* you doing?"

"Just fine, Edgar, just fine."

"Well, you sure look like you're doing fine." Then, leaning forward, Edgar asked the critical question. "How's that leg doing?"

And with that cue, Aunt Dot launched into a ninety-second description of her leg that was surpassed in oratorical brilliance only by Jack Kennedy's "Ask not what your country can do for you. . . ."

In terms of creating partnership feelings with customers, Edgar left the stamp machine at the starting line.

Does this mean that the "stamp machines" of the world don't count? That technology has no place in customer partnerships? On the contrary! It just means that caring is critical.

The Chevrolet Roadside Assistance Program, for example, makes good use of technology to improve customer loyalty. Call the 800 number, give the person at the other end of the line your vehicle identification number, and she has a computer screen that gives her more information about your particular car than you would ever even dream of knowing.

Tell her you left Kingston, Rhode Island, about an hour ago and are heading toward Stamford, Connecticut, on I-95. She can pull up another screen that gives the names of the two or three closest dealerships, the service manager at each, and directions on how to get there! Explain that your car is making an irregular ker-thump noise that turns into a regular ker-thwack noise at forty-five miles per hour, and she'll have two or three possibilities of what might be wrong.

Customer service representatives know all that because they have an enormous data base at their disposal. They know your car because they've been in classes and examined cars. They seem knowledgeable because they are. They're all college graduates.

But they also care. I've listened to them talk to customers who need help. And they demonstrate the same concern and care for the driver on the other end of the line that Edgar demonstrated toward Aunt Dot.

And in that caring, they forge a partnership with the owner — a partnership that leads to a repurchase rate of 90 percent among Chevrolet owners who call the Roadside Assistance Program — compared with an industry average of 38 percent.

So if you want to double your customer loyalty with a low-tech approach like Edgar's, create partnerships by caring. And if you want to double your customer loyalty with a high-tech approach like Chevrolet's Roadside Assistance Program, create partnerships by caring.

200 And most important, make sure that you demonstrate caring for all your partners: life, family, friends — and customers.

Chapter 26

WHEN PARTNERS CRY "WOLF!"

by Kristin Anderson

*T*HERE IS A MOVEMENT UNDERWAY to rewrite the fables and fairy tales we snuggled up to as young children. It seems the rewriters now view them as too old, too sexist, and too violent to speak correctly to kids today. I'm hoping the movement fails.

Yes, some of the stories need new readers and new interpretations. But they do not need new words or new plots.

Take, for instance, the classic story of the little boy who cried "wolf." Ever since my tenth-grade physics teacher told about a summer spent sheepherding in Wyoming, I have felt great empathy with the little boy in the fable. I picture him alone, very bored, and smelling nothing but sheep. He can look down and watch the villagers busily working in the fields — together.

"This is just too much," he thinks. Then the idea hits him. "Wolf!" he cries.

It's much better than he had even imagined. The villagers immediately stop working. They dash to get pitchforks and scythes, then storm up the mountain. You might even imagine the little boy joyfully going down on one knee, raising a clenched fist, squinting his eyes, and uttering "Yessss!" as if he suddenly had the lead role in *Home Alone III*!

Sure, the people are mad when they find no wolf and no danger. But angry villagers are still a lot better company than smelly sheep. The villagers depart. Left alone, the shepherd boy is soon lonely again. So — again he cries, "Wolf!" and the cycle repeats itself. Each time the boy has to cry "Wolf!" louder and longer. And each time the village people come more slowly. Finally, they don't come at all.

But the wolf does. And the sheep die.

"Don't cry 'wolf'" means don't give false alarms. It's the moral of the story and the reason it is told to us when we are young. But this story, like most, has another lesson to teach: Stop listening and your sheep will get eaten.

After all, the villagers were the big losers in this story. The boy? Well, the tragedy guaranteed no more smelly, lonely summers spent with sheep. Seems to me that's a rather large mark in the "plus" column!

"All right, but so what?" you say. "It's cute, but who cares?" We all should! Too often we are like the villagers. We send our partners — our customers and colleagues — off to watch the sheep. "I don't want to hear from you unless you've got a *real* problem," we subtly communicate. We have important work in the fields — no time to make small talk or to empathize with the olfactory challenge of a summer with sheep. That's just the way it is.

We tune out the complaints, the communication, until our sheep are eaten.

Even then, we tend to blame our partners — just as the village blamed the little boy. And our partners? They're soon off dealing with more empathetic service providers. And buying from more sensitive sellers.

How do we prevent this tragedy? How do we protect our sheep? In a word: Listen.

Listen for more than the words. Does "Wolf!" really mean "Pay attention, don't take me for granted," or "Watch out, threat approaching"? The narrow vocabulary of "Fine," "Satisfied," "Did not fully meet expectations" on customer-feedback forms never tells the entire story.

Listen every time, even when you think you know the words and their meaning. Listen when it is the first time and when it is the five hundredth.

We don't need to rewrite the fables and fairy tales that are part of our culture. But we do need to reread them — and listen for new meanings beyond the old words.

203

Chapter 27

PARTNERSHIP EXPECTATIONS

by Karen Revill

O YOU HAVE YOUR receipt?" asked the clerk, looking over her glasses like a judge questioning a criminal. The question sounded as though the clerk actually hoped the answer would be no so the customer could be zapped.

The customer answered in her most pitiful tone. "No, but I was just here this morning buying this sweater. When I got home, I realized it didn't match the skirt in my closet. Can't you please check the cash-register tape? I was here at eleven o'clock." The honest face waited for the verdict.

"You should have known that you could not return merchandise without a receipt. You'll have to bring it back *with* your receipt." You could almost hear a gavel rap and the words "Next case!" spoken in the background.

We all have expectations in our relationships — whether with parents, spouse, friends, or customers. Expectations are tools to avoid all the "You should have knowns" in our lives. Since my mom worked, my sister and I were supervised by my aunt. Our childhood, like most childhoods, was made difficult by a constant stream of unanticipated, unannounced, "You should have known" rules for everything. When customers get treated like children, there's little chance for successful partnering.

I once worked as the manager of the shoe department in an elite women's clothing store. During my first few weeks I came face to face with the opposite of great expectations. Some customers arrived at 8:55 p.m., when no one wanted to wait on them since it could result in working past the 9:00 p.m. closing time. Some customers forgot their credit cards. Instead of looking up the card number, clerks would send customers away — to shop elsewhere.

There are two parts to successful partnership expectations. First, expectations need to be clear: the more vagueness and uncertainty, the more chance for later disappointment. This means that the service provider must work hard to be precise and up front about "This is what I expect of you." The service provider must also encourage customers to be clear about their expectations. It takes mutual effort to have clear expectations. Mutuality takes straight talk from both sides of the relationship.

The second part of successful partnership expectations is doing what you say you're going to do. If the sign says "Open at 9 a.m.," customers deserve to be served at nine rather than having to wait for the "computer to warm up." "Closed at nine" is not the same as "Clerks go home at nine." Clear expectations are like promises. They are made to be kept until they are changed — together.

How much do we really expect from our customers? Are they always required to be the brave ones? Do

we act in a manner that teaches customers that what
we say as the truth is "nothing but the truth"? Do we stand
in our customers' shoes and view service expectations
from their point of view? Do we help our customers see
expectations from our point of view? Do we sometimes
set our customers up for "You should have known" dis-
appointments?

One summer I received a tennis racket and tennis
balls for my birthday. While there were courts near our
home, they did not come with tennis partners. I was over-
eager to try out my new gift, and the nearest partner was
the side of our house. Despite previous warnings from my
mother of "no balls thrown at the side of the house," eager-
ness overrode obedience! "Besides," I thought to myself,
"I'm not going to hurt anything." I began playing a set
with the house.

Very soon there was a tennis ball on the living-
room floor, a tennis player with a strong forehand in the
front yard, and shattered glass in between. Even though
the rule was orally explicit, the temptation had been too
strong to resist.

Service expectations need to be designed to be easy
to follow. We need to view our service offerings with the
question, "We know what we expect, but how will customers react to our expectations?" Are service rules written
in such dictatorial, judgmental tones that they invite rebellious "I'll show you" behavior from customers?

Are service rules so vague that they entrap customers in innocent errors? Service expectations need to
be devoid of "gotchas." Gotchas are like telling a child she
can have a toy if she is good, but neglecting to give her a
time frame. When the child asks for her due, she is hit
with "You're past the time limit." Children and customers
are incapable of mind reading.

Expectations need precision balanced with compassion. The customer is always right, since he is always
the customer and can render you bankrupt. However, the
customer is not always *correct*. When normal, reasonable

incorrectness runs head-on into the exactness of expectations, compassion is needed.

I recently had a problem with a notebook computer. I first called the electronics store where the computer was purchased. Over the phone, the store concluded that my computer problem was the battery. However, the store had no replacement batteries in stock. I contacted the manufacturer, who sent a replacement. The computer still failed to work.

Putting the old battery back in, I took the computer to the repair shop, along with the new battery. It took forever to get the computer repaired and returned. The repair shop also concluded that my problem had nothing to do with the battery. So now I had a new, unused battery I did not need.

I again contacted the manufacturer to arrange the return of the replacement battery they had sent earlier. That's when I was informed of their thirty-day return policy. I carefully explained that the repairs had taken longer than expected. The company steadfastly stood on its policy. I explained that I was not at any time told of their policy and had nothing in any correspondence about their cutoff time; I had not received an invoice because I had billed it to a credit card, and there was nothing about the policy on the packing slip. The company would not budge.

Do I respect this company's policy? Yes. Do I respect this company's compassion? You know the answer to that!

You may be thinking, "But some customers can never be satisfied, no matter how hard you work to meet their expectations." There are occasional unrealizable expectations. However, there can be a payoff even if you "go down in flames" dealing with the occasional difficult customer.

My job as a shoe-department manager gave me a unique window on the world of customer expectations. One very busy Saturday morning a woman rushed into the store, stood in front of me, and loudly demanded, "Is

anyone going to help me?" I quickly moved into her line of
fire. "What can I help you find?" I inquired with "super
friendly" in my tone. "I need a gold metallic pump in a
size 7, now!" she snapped. "My husband is double parked."

I quickly went to the stockroom knowing that the
"getting close to Christmas" condition of our stock made
it unlikely I would find exactly what she wanted. Finding
no size 7, I pulled a 7½ plus a couple of possibilities in
similar shoes, size 7. The 7½ failed to fit; the options were
not to her liking.

"Well, what are you going to do about it?" she
loudly asked, letting the entire store in on her displeas-
ure. My "We can call other stores" suggestion collided
with her "I don't have time to wait" response. After several of my attempts to appease her, she left in a huff. Other
customers quickly moved in to console me. I was moved.
I had lost a customer in my "go the extra mile" efforts to
respond to expectations, but I gained several replacements
along the way.

Partnership expectations are key to giving partners
a clear path for action. They minimize disappointment
and maximize understanding. They take planning and
clarity at the start. They require discipline and commitment in the middle. And they need reasonableness and
compassion at the end.

Chapter 28

POETIC PARTNERSHIP

by Nancy Rainey Bell

I WONDER WHEN it all began,
no doubt in my small home-town land;
in Walnut Ridge where I once had
a loving sister, mom, and dad.

I watched my family come and go.
My mom would sew, my dad would mow;
they demonstrated special love,
and friendship close as hand and glove.

"Partnership" was their advice,
the route to my own wedding rice;
I hoped some day he'd come along,
I knew not how; he'd sing a song.

Then one day in a distant state
I met him there; he said, "Let's date."
Pure joy it was to dance and sing;
I still admire my wedding ring.

For thirty most exciting years
we laughed, we smiled, we shed some tears;
candor was our useful tool,
fair play was our constant rule.

We've worked and learned and played a lot —
we even have a special tot.
The years have come and gone so fast,
by now we know our bond is cast.

Chip's the one from out of state —
Georgia birthed this lifelong mate;
Bilijack's the tot who came,
a sharp young man, yet hard to tame.

In this good book on partnerships
I'm happy to provide some tips:
hang tough, be straight and also nice;
with care, you'll have your personal "rice."

Words like "thanks" and "help" and "please,"
said from your heart, make bonds a breeze;
like mates and friends, your patrons too
will share great joy and revenue.

Chapter 29

PARTNERSHIP MEASUREMENT

I WAS EIGHTY-NINE MINUTES into a ninety-minute speech. Just as I was reaching my stirring last sentence, a hand went up three rows from the front. "This all sounds great," the person said loudly, "but how do you measure customer partnership?" The squint-eyed naysayer sat back with arms tightly crossed, waiting to set me straight with a discourse on quantification and statistical process-control methods.

Everything in me cried out to say, "Check with me at the break." The Peck's Bad Boy side of me wanted to ask, "How do you measure the success of your marriage?" I even thought of saying, "By using the R-test of

Duncan's Multiple-Range Factor Analysis carried to the .001 level of significance, you can create a bimodal distribution that should do the trick." But instead I fended him off with some fast talk.

My strong desire to get offstage aside, the question is a relevant one in an era when corporate boards keep a quarter-to-quarter watch on ROI, ROE, and P-E ratios. A personal faith in partnerships can be a business touchstone only as far as there are facts and figures to justify it.

The economics of partnership is compelling. Energy spent on retaining customers has a higher return than energy spent acquiring customers, by at least five-to-one — some researchers say much more. Customers who feel loyal to a service provider spend more over time and tell more people about their positive experience. There is no better marketing and advertisement than acclamations delivered by happy customers to associates. The partnership level of loyalty is the pinnacle of customer commitment to a service provider.

Measurability of this sort *can* be, and *is,* a valuable tool in monitoring progress. But myopically seized upon, it can also be a time-wasting, cover-your-backside, proof-seeking effort. As my partner Tom Connellan is fond of saying, "Anything not worth measuring is not worth measuring well."

My need to balance both bottom-line and life-line reasons for customer partnering was powerfully supported recently in one of excellence guru Tom Peters's newspaper columns. He cited John Steinbeck's description of a fishing expedition:

> The Mexican sierra has 17 plus 15 plus nine spines in the dorsal fin. These can easily be counted. But if the sierra strikes hard on the line so that our hands are burned, if the fish sounds and nearly escapes and finally comes in over the rail, his colors pulsing and

his tail beating in the air, a whole new relational externality has come into being — an entity which is more than the sum of the fish plus the fisherman.

The only way to count the spines of the sierra unaffected by this second relational reality is to sit in a laboratory, open an evil-smelling jar, remove a stiff colorless fish from the formalin solution, count the spines and write the truth. . . . There you have recorded a reality which cannot be assailed — probably the least important reality concerning either the fish or yourself.

There are no easy answers to partnership measurability. And if the dollar benefits were all there were to recommend a partnering attitude to your business, it would be a weak recommendation indeed. To justify partnering solely on the basis of the economic argument is to cheapen and blunt the experience of partnering for those who must deal with the customer one day at a time, day in and day out.

The salesperson, for example, who learns great customer relations techniques for the sole purpose of economic return never truly escapes the box marked "Techniquing the Customer to Achieve an End"; not in the salesperson's mind — and not in his customer's.

The price of inauthentic partnering is high; the drain of unrequited emotional energy can provoke burnout, disaffection, and brittleness. There is an emotional cost associated with customer caring. But that price is a bargain compared with the hollowness of shallow service encounters and the lethargy of routine responses.

Partnerships nurture strength in all parties involved. The strength partners experience is real, valued, and reciprocal. That it cannot be calibrated in pounds per square inch matters not to partners passionately involved.

I can say with assurance that many important aspects of successful customer partnership are not effectively measured with the tools you might use to judge the financial impact of a merger or a new computer. Using economic tools to measure the relational aspects of service quality is, to quote my friend Tony Putman, "like trying to drive a nail with a B flat!"

Or as Marilyn Ferguson said in her book *The Aquarian Conspiracy,*

> In our lives and in our cultural institutions we have been poking at qualities with tools designed to detect quantities. By what yardstick do you measure a shadow, a candle flame? What does an intelligence test measure? Where in the medical armamentarium is the will to live? How big is an intention? How heavy is grief, how deep is love?

216

The
"Riding Off into the Sunset"
Part

T HE SUN IS STARTING TO SET over the water at Cedar Creek Lake, Texas, and my computer screen is getting more difficult to see. Besides, Texas sunsets are tough competition!

Writing this has been a great experience for me. In a profound and personal way, the process has helped me sort out what I believe about customers and partnerships. I hope you enjoyed and found beneficial our journey together from page one.

Before my grandfather passed away at age eighty-six, I asked him how his era was different from mine. It was in the late '60s and I was preparing to go to war. "Our day was harder," he said, "but happier." The "harder" part I had expected; the "happier" part surprised me. I asked him for his reason. Looking out across a field of freshly plowed ground, he slowly answered, "Seems like back then we had more neighbors."

We need partnerships today — those neighbor-like relationships that honor service at a caring level.

Without a lot of partnerships, we will continue to see newspaper front pages that scream stories of discord and disdain.

True partners remain loyal through good times *and* bad, through healthy moments and sickly madness, and through joyful wins and disappointing mistakes. Such commitment starts and continues with the expression of a partnership orientation: gift giving, leaps of faith, shared dreams, honesty, floating reciprocity, and the continual quest for graceful dealings.

The by-product of customer partnerships is more than loyalty. The deeper consequence is that partnerships foster lives of peace, joy, and contribution.

Partnership does not happen solely through good intentions. It starts with the courageous act to more passionately connect. And it starts with a single encounter — your next one.

❝ *Only connect.* ❞
— E. M. Forster, *Howards End*

SOURCES

*Page
no.*

xii Frederick F. Reichheld and W. Earl Sasser Jr., "Zero Defections: Quality Comes to Services," *Harvard Business Review,* September–October 1990, pp. 105-111.

32 Clarence Jordan, *The Cotton Patch Version of Luke and Acts* (Clinton, New Jersey: New Win Publishing, 1969), pp. 46–47. Distributed by Koinonia Center, Americus, Georgia.

40 Robert A. Peterson, "Measuring Customer Satisfaction: Fact or Artifact" (University of Texas Working Paper). Quoted in "What's Love Got to Do with It," by Ron Zemke, *The Service Edge Newsletter,* January 1991, p. 8.

56 "Trust Your Customer," *Success,* January/February 1994, p. 26.

63 Leonard L. Berry and A. Parasuraman, *Marketing Services: Competing Through Quality* (New York: The Free Press, 1991), p. 16.

79 The Country Kitchen purpose statement comes from their menu. Used by permission.

81 "Survival of the Smartest," *Inc.,* December 1993, p. 78.

83 Chapter 11 is based on a series of interviews conducted by the author with John Longstreet.

93 Chapter 12 is based on a series of interviews conducted by the author with Sharon Decker.

111   Theodore Levitt, "After the Sale Is Over . . . ," *Harvard Business Review*, September–October 1983, pp. 88–94.

112   Ibid., p. 89.

113   *Consumer Complaint Handling in America: An Update Study, Part III,* a research project undertaken by Technical Assistance Research Programs Institute (TARP) at the request of the U.S. Office of Consumer Affairs, February 26, 1986. John Goodman is president of TARP Institute.

114   Jerry B. Harvey, *The Abilene Paradox and Other Meditations on Management* (New York: Lexington Books, 1988).

116   Peter Matthews (ed.), *The Guinness Book of Records 1994* (New York: Guinness Publishing Ltd., 1993).

173   Benjamin Schneider and David E. Bowen, "Employee and Customer Perceptions of Service in Banks: Replication and Extension," *Journal of Applied Psychology* 70, no. 3 (1985), pp. 423–433.

181   Max De Pree, *Leadership Is an Art* (New York: Doubleday, 1989), p. 9.

185   Nicholas Imparato and Oren Harari, *Jumping the Curve: Innovation and Strategic Choice in an Age of Transition* (San Francisco: Jossey-Bass, 1994), p. 187.

189   Karl Albrecht and Ron Zemke, *Service America! Doing Business in the New Economy* (Homewood, Ill.: Business One Irwin, 1985). Ron Zemke and Dick Schaaf, *The Service Edge: One Hundred One Companies That Profit from Customer Care* (New York: NAL-Dutton, 1990). Ron Zemke and Thomas Kramlinger, *Figuring Things Out: A Trainer's Guide to Needs and Task Analysis* (Reading, Mass.: Addison-Wesley, 1982). Ron Zemke and Chip R. Bell, *Service Wisdom: Creating and Maintaining the Customer Service Edge* (Minneapolis, Minn.: Lakewood Books, 1989). Chip R. Bell and Ron Zemke, *Managing Knock Your Socks Off Service* (New York: AMACOM, 1992). Kristin Anderson and Ron Zemke, *Delivering Knock Your Socks Off Service* (New York: AMACOM, 1991). Ron Zemke and Thomas K. Connellan, *Sustaining Knock Your Socks Off Service* (New York: AMACOM, 1993). Kristin Anderson and Ron Zemke, *Knock Your Socks Off Answers* (New York: AMACOM, 1995).

190   Thomas K. Connellan, *How to Grow People into Self Starters* (Ann Arbor, Mich.: Achievement Institute, 1988). Kristin Anderson, *Great Customer Service on the Telephone* (New York: AMACOM, 1992).

214   Quoted from "Thinking in Wholes," by Tom Peters, *San Jose Mercury News,* July 9, 1993. The extract originally appeared in *Sea of Cortez: A Leisurely Journal of Travel and Research* by John Steinbeck and Edward F. Ricketts (New York: Viking Press, 1941), p. 2.

216   Marilyn Ferguson, *The Aquarian Conspiracy* (Los Angeles: J. P. Tarcher, 1980), p. 176.

Small portions of *Customers As Partners* have previously appeared in various professional journals, including *Services* (June 1990), *AFSM International* (July 1991 and February 1992), *Executive Excellence* (July 1991 and August 1993), *Mobius* (Summer 1990 and April 1992), *Training* (May 1990), *Association Management* (March 1994), and *Quality Digest* (January 1994).

For
Your Continued
Learning

*I*F ANYONE EVER ASKED ME to name and describe a few written resources helpful to learning about customers as partners, I would say, "None, you don't learn to partner by reading." But then the rational side of me would remind the flippant side of me: "Get down off your high horse; you just wrote a book on the subject!" So for your rational side, below are a few written resources that may give you helpful hints for rekindling, renewing, and refining partnerships.

Bell, Chip R., and Ron Zemke. *Managing Knock Your Socks Off Service.* New York: AMACOM, 1992.

My partner and I wrote this book for managers who sought ideas on how to lead people who served customers. The concepts and ideas are laced with a partnership orientation. It contains countless tips and techniques useful in helping service people dazzle their internal and/or external customers with service excellence.

Block, Peter. *Stewardship: Choosing Service over Self-Interest.* San Francisco: Berrett-Koehler Publishers, 1993.

Peter Block spawned this book from the same perspective he used to craft *The Empowered Manager* (San Francisco: Jossey-Bass Publishers, 1987). It is an invitation to deep reform in how we manage relationships in organizations. If Thomas Jefferson had written a book about democracy in *corporate* America, it would have been a declaration like this.

Covey, Stephen R. *Principle-Centered Leadership.* New York: Summit Books, 1990.

Stephen Covey has cut a deep dent into eliminating corporate greed, cynicism, and selfishness. This book, along with his best-selling *The Seven Habits of Highly Effective People* (New York: Simon and Schuster, 1989), delivers a wake-up call to leaders to return to the natural laws and governing values most of us learned and honored as children.

De Pree, Max. *Leadership Jazz.* New York: Doubleday, 1992.

There are a lot of great books written by consultants and professional writers. This one is crafted by the CEO of a successful furniture maker. As such, it combines the realism of a "message from the barricades" with the soul of a leader's search for meaning. Max has much to say about the role of values in leadership and in life. His poetic prose reminds us that the solid grounding of organizational life is best lived with purpose and contribution.

Gilbreath, Robert D. *Escape from Management Hell.* San Francisco: Berrett-Koehler Publishers, 1993.

Imagine this: Twelve executives crash their commuter plane returning from a boondoggle and end up in hell. Their only escape is to tell a strong "make me laugh and make me learn" story to the devil. This combination has the making of humorous parables on contemporary work life. The powerful fables left me reflecting on the true meaning of leadership responsibility, whether a citizen or an organization, a community or a family.

Harvey, Jerry B. *The Abilene Paradox and Other Meditations on Management.* New York: Lexington Books, 1988.

The cover describes this book as "compassionate insights into the craziness of organizational life." Jerry wraps "slam on brakes" stories around deep and important concepts in making organizations work. His pithy insights point the way to soul searching and reality checking. As Willard Scott said of a favorite book, "If you only read two books this year, read this one twice!"

Levitt, Theodore. *Thinking about Management.* New York: Free Press, 1991.

The patron saint of thinking managers and managers who think about — and respect — their customers has a lot to say about the running of organizations. "Business is about two things, money and customers," says Levitt. "And, of course," he adds, "taking care of the second takes care of the first almost automatically."

Melohn, Tom. *The New Partnership.* Essex Junction, Vermont: Oliver Wight Publications, 1994.

We are at the edge of a new paradigm in business leadership. Smart leaders are discovering that their effectiveness lies in caring, not controlling, and in partnering, not parenting. Tom's experiences as CEO, owner, and "head sweeper" of North American Tool & Die were first heralded on the PBS-TV documentary *In Search of Excellence.* He looks back on his twelve-year odyssey with NATD and writes from the heart lessons important for any leader. His blueprint for leadership can assist others wishing to bring the partnership orientation to people management.

Williams, Margery. *The Velveteen Rabbit.* New York: Avon Books, 1975.

I know — you read it to your kids when they were toddlers. Now, go back and read it again for yourself and the partners in your life.

INDEX

Index

THANKS

BOOK WRITING HAS TO BE one of the purest crucibles for partnership. The process repeatedly tests the limits of relationships. The product is the benefit of the depths of interdependence. I have many to thank for their elasticity, their candor, and their leaps of faith with me.

Ron Zemke has been my primary shepherd. He encouraged me to solo this book when I sought the security of a joint byline. He read draft after draft after draft, always adding his wisdom and encouragement. And he was always willing to join me in the laboratory of dialogue to test ideas in their embryonic stage and refine them toward maturity. He is also my friend.

Steve Piersanti has created a world-class publishing organization. Steve lives partnership. And that orientation permeates Berrett-Koehler Publishers. Having worked with several publishers over the last fifteen years, I can honestly say none have even come close to his proactive integrity, his supportive inspiration, and his vision for how enterprises can be. He has assembled an incredibly talented, energetic team.

Leslie Stephen gave me affirming support and creative suggestions as the project leader for Bard & Stephen, the same level of excellence she did on my second

Thanks

book in 1982. Chris Lee and Jeff Morris were my primary language engineers. Their editing helped smooth the edges and sharpen the message on what must have seemed like random note cards. Suzanne Pustejovsky's artful text design perfectly captured the tone and spirit of the partnership message.

I was also assisted by others who read some or all of the manuscript and offered helpful suggestions: Tom Connellan, Kristin Anderson, George Morrisey, Oren Harari, Ted Cocheu, Marcia Daszko, Greg Wood, Larry Davis, Glenn Kiser, and Tony Putman. Jill Bernstein and Jim Cadwell of Bernstein/Cadwell in Phoenix provided innovative and provocative ideas and assistance on publicity for the book.

Finally, the most important partner in my life, Nancy Rainey Bell, gave me many gifts. Every writer births a book through the ancient process of sleepless nights, long stares at a blank computer screen, days when every page is hurled at the trash can, interspersed with moments of insight and flow. This sometimes lonely process was made more peaceful through her support. This often frustrating course was made more joyful through the freedom she ensured. This soul-searching creation was made more worthy through her inspiration.

To all of you, thank you from the bottom of my heart!

Chip

Chip R. Bell
Dallas, Texas
May 1994

ABOUT THE AUTHOR

CHIP R. BELL IS A TEXAN-IN-TRAINING who now lives in Dallas but spends most of his time flying around North America and Europe telling tall tales and exaggerating his achievements.

He grew up on a farm near Alamo, Georgia, and has served as a service-quality consultant to numerous major organizations, including GTE, Shell Oil, Nabisco, IBM, Blockbuster Video, Eli Lilly, GE, MCI, Price Waterhouse, Ryder, First Union, and Marriott. He is the author or coauthor of nine books, including *Managing Knock Your Socks Off Service* and *Service Wisdom*. He has been married for thirty years to Nancy R. Bell, a former high-school principal who is now a lawyer-in-training. They have a twenty-three-year-old son, Bilijack, a clumsy Shetland sheepdog, and a hostile black cat. One of his life goals is to set the State of Texas record for the largest number of catfish caught on a cane pole in a single hour.

Chip can be contacted at

Performance Research Associates, Inc.
25 Highland Park #100
Dallas, Texas 75205-2785
Phone 214-522-5777   fax 214-691-7591